You Can Make a Difference

You Can Make a Difference

14 Principles
For Influencing Lives

GARY R. COLLINS

ZondervanPublishingHouse

Grand Rapids, Michigan

A Division of HarperCollinsPublishers

You Can Make a Difference
Copyright © 1992 by Gary R. Collins

Requests for information should be addressed to:
Zondervan Publishing House
Grand Rapids, Michigan 49530

Library of Congress Cataloging-in-Publication Data

Collins, Gary R.
    You can make a difference / Gary R. Collins.
        p. cm.
    ISBN 0-310-57380-7
    1. Christian life, 1960– I. Title.
BV4501.C6863   1992
248.4—dc20   91–42010
                                                            CIP

Edited by Bruce and Becky Durost Fish
Interior designed by Bob Hudson
Cover designed by Lecy Design

Printed in the United States of America

92 93 94 95 96 / DH / 10 9 8 7 6 5 4 3 2 1

To Arthur and Berniece Matthews
of Portland, Oregon

True difference makers
whose impact continues

Contents

Part Three
Everyday Difference Makers

Acknowledgments

"No matter what accomplishments you make, somebody helps you."

These wise words of Althea Gibson certainly apply to anyone who writes a book. They are very much true of me.

Many people have helped with the production of this book, including those whose stories are told in the following pages. I am grateful to all of them, and want to express special thanks to the following people who read and critiqued portions of the manuscript prior to publication: Tim Clinton, Lynn Collins, Mark Mittelberg, Steve Sandage, Ken Wessner, Sandra Vander Zicht, and especially my wife, Julie Collins.

Part One

Who Can Be a Difference Maker?

1

What Makes a Difference Maker?

Mama, come quick! There's fire!"

The tiny, terror-filled voices catapulted Sukey from her bed. She grabbed her two girls, rushed from the room, and stumbled into the hall already aglow from flames near the staircase. Churning black smoke stung her eyes and blocked her vision. She prayed fervently, groping her way toward the door.

The night air was cool, almost invigorating, as Sukey dashed barefoot across the damp grass with the girls. Crackling orange flames leapt into the jet black sky behind her and cast an eerie glow on the faces of neighbors who were running to help.

Suddenly a small head appeared in a second floor window, silhouetted against a background of solid fire. It was Jackie, Sukey's special son, the five-year-old who seemed most like his mother.

Without hesitation, two courageous neighbors dashed toward the inferno. One braced himself against the stucco wall. The other clambered to the first man's shoulders and grabbed Jackie by the hair. The boy fell to the ground and scrambled to his mother an instant before the roof collapsed.

The second floor quickly gave way under the weight. Then, while Sukey and the neighbors watched in stunned silence, the walls crumbled slowly—almost majestically—into heaps of rubble, sparks, and soot.

Sukey lost everything that night: the house that was

home, books that she loved, the devotional guide for her children that she had been writing for months. But the fire was only one of many set-backs that clouded Sukey's life. A brilliant woman who taught herself Greek and Hebrew, Sukey had longed to go to a university, but she lived in a time when higher education was only for men. Financial problems and a shaky marriage plagued her adult life. Children came too frequently, and the sickly ones died. Sukey was often weak and ill, struggling alone to raise the children while her husband was gone for months at a time.

After the house was rebuilt, Sukey began a Sunday evening service for her children. At first one or two neighbors dropped by to join the worship, but soon over two hundred villagers squeezed into the house every week to hear the prayers and messages. No one was surprised when the local curate objected. His empty sermons said little to the people who came to his almost empty church. In contrast, Sukey's crowded evening devotionals were meeting spiritual needs. But they were led by an unordained woman who was treading into the domain of a weak church with a sanctimonious clergy. Sukey was instructed to stop.

Within a few years, Sukey's children began to leave home. Some moved into poor marriages. Others went to school far from home when they were much too young. Jackie was eleven when he left for prep school in London. His brother Charles was less than eight. Sukey began to suffer from debilitating bouts of depression.

When she died at age seventy-three, did Sukey feel that her life had been a failure? The passing years had not been easy. Her dreams had never been realized. Jackie and Charles had gone into missions but returned home dejected and discouraged.

Yet Sukey's prayers, spiritual example, Bible teachings, and dedicated mothering had made an indelible impact on her children and would make a lasting impact on the world.

Charles and his brother Jackie—better known as John Wesley—were used by God to start a great revival that changed thousands of lives, influenced the course of British history, and led to the founding of the Methodist church. Throughout his life John Wesley traveled thousands of miles on horseback, preaching the Gospel and leading people to Christ. Charles composed over six thousand hymns, many of which we still sing today. The Wesley brothers were difference makers.

Sukey, better known as Susanna Wesley, was a difference maker too. And she never knew it.[1]

You Can Be a Difference Maker

The pages of this book have one basic message: Everybody, including you, can make a difference in this world. You don't have to be a Wesley, a model parent, a preacher, a book writer, or a success in your work. You don't have to be perfect, saintly, rich, comfortable with people, highly educated, in good health, exceptionally intelligent, oozing self-confidence, or even unusual. Regardless of who you are, where you live, or how often you have failed, you still can make a difference. You are never too young, too old, too insecure, too poorly educated, too infirm, or too imperfect. The following pages will describe famous difference makers, like the Wesleys, but there will be other examples of unknown, ordinary people—maybe people like you—whose lives and words have made a difference.

All of us know about great men and women whose vision, leadership, and acts of courage swayed empires and changed history. Some, like Hitler and Stalin, are remembered for their ruthless cruelty and self-serving lust for power. These difference makers did incredible harm. In contrast, people like Churchill and Eisenhower were difference makers who courageously ended wars and encouraged whole nations during dark days of difficulty and destruction.

But there aren't very many Churchills or Eisenhowers in this world. There are few Billy Grahams or Mother Teresas in the church. Most of us will never reach positions of great power, prominence, and influence. Some will be successful, as the world counts success, but at the end of life, our names are unlikely to be included among the great difference makers of history.

More of us might be like my mother. A few years ago, her world collapsed when my father died. Because of failing eyesight she could no longer drive, so the family car was sold. Arthritis slowed her walk and kept her from venturing too far from the little apartment where she lived by herself. After a while, the previously-solicitous neighbors went back to their busy lives and left her alone to cope with loneliness and widowhood. Her attitude has always been good and my mother rarely complains, but she's puzzled by one thing.

"I don't know why I'm still here," she says. "I can't do anything. I have to depend on other people if I want to get groceries or go anywhere. My life doesn't make much of a difference to anybody. The only thing I can do is pray."

So the lady has become a prayer warrior. Her intercessions flow continually to heaven, and many of us are confident that her prayers make a significant difference.

But my mother still wonders what she is accomplishing, and I suspect many of us have similar misgivings. We want to make a difference in this world, but we doubt that we will ever succeed. Sometimes we don't even bother to try.

Why Bother?

Imagine what life would be like teaching in a high school that one writer described as "an overcrowded old pile of remarkable history and innumerable problems." Planted in a violent, drug-infested, inner-city neighborhood, the school doesn't have enough classrooms, teachers, or books. But there are plenty of unmotivated, glassy-eyed students.

Far away in their plush offices, crotchety pencil pushers plan the school budgets and set policy. These are unlovable educators, evaluated by one critic as "heedless when not selfish, petty when not despotic in the wielding of whatever power they possess." They are part of a school system "with practically no quality control or accountability for students or staff, lacking in obvious essentials (though well-supplied with bureaucrats), mindlessly rigid in its procedures, and profoundly unjust in some of its basic policies."

Jessica Siegel was almost thirty when she entered this system as an English teacher. She taught a variety of courses at Seward High School, advised the school paper, and gave unselfishly to her students. Often Jessica would work into the night or get up before dawn to prepare lessons and plan classes. Sometimes she would stay after school to give extra help or to guide students with their educational and career plans. She was in touch with their families and spent hours at home grading papers. Few people paid much attention to what Jessica Siegel was doing or to the difference she was making—at least in a few lives. She might never have been known beyond her small circle of friends and students had Samuel Freedman not entered her life.

Freedman is a former *New York Times* reporter who decided to spend a year observing and writing about life in the local high school where Ms. Siegel taught her classes. The reporter interviewed students and sat in the classrooms. Sometimes he watched the teachers, many of whom were frustrated or bored and just putting in time. Perhaps Samuel Freedman hoped to write a book that would tell the inspiring story of one determined teacher who was making a difference despite her surroundings and frustrations. But when classes let out in the late spring and the reporter went off to write his book, the teacher made a distressing decision.

Jessica Siegel quit.

Well-intentioned motivational speakers or possibility thinkers might say she was a deserter. Surely she knew that good teachers are rare and desperately needed—especially in troubled schools. Why would she turn her back on those few motivated but trapped high school kids who really did want to make something of their lives? Didn't Jessica Siegel want her life to count? Why would some more charitable observers overlook the resignation but applaud the former teacher for lasting as long as she did?[2]

Jessica Siegel wanted to make a difference. In a few lives she succeeded, but her story of frustration raises a basic question about difference making. Why bother?

There are many reasons why we should bother to be difference makers, but three are of utmost importance. All three apply to people like you and me. Each of the three gives us a reason to be concerned about making a difference as we pass through this life.

The first reason is that *our world depends on it*. Society, including the neighborhoods where we live, would never survive if people lived like islands, untouched by others and uninvolved with individuals other than themselves or their own families. Generations of sociologists and anthropologists have shown how people live in groups that support and need each other.

What would this world be like if there were no good Samaritans, no caring people-helpers who refused to let ethnic differences, diverse nationalities, religious distinctions, or busy schedules get in the way of helping somebody in need? The biblical parable only lets us imagine how the wounded man, robbed, beaten, and half dead, must have felt when he woke up in the inn and discovered that a stranger, a foreigner, had stopped to help him.[3]

Our world is filled with violence, insensitivity, greed, hatred, and selfishness. The newspapers show that every day. But the same newspapers show how whole nations rise to help victims of earthquakes, tornadoes, devastating floods, indescribable hunger, personal tragedies, and the pain of war. Like the priest and the Levite, some people pass by when they see an accident on the freeway, but others stop to help in whatever way they can. When disasters strike some individuals keep their wallets zipped shut, but others give generously even when their own budgets are tight. Despite a core of human sin and self-centered attitudes, there is something in most of us that reaches out to help when there is human need. In some places there are legitimate fears because getting involved could mean getting hurt, but even crime-infested neighborhoods have caring individuals who are committed to helping each other, whatever the cost. Without these compassionate people, the world would disintegrate into chaos.

A second reason we must bother to be difference makers is that *our fulfillment in life depends on it*. Jesus never told his audience how the Good Samaritan felt when he left the inn and continued on his journey. Might he have gone on his way, not buoyed by sinful pride or self-righteous vanity, but feeling fulfilled because he had done something useful? His travels had been interrupted, but his actions had made a difference.

A deep sense of satisfaction and fulfillment floods into our lives when we take the time and energy to do something worthwhile. We don't want to fritter away our years, only to conclude at the end that our lives didn't make a difference to anybody.[4]

The third reason to be a difference maker is that *God expects it*. At the time of creation, Adam was placed in the Garden of Eden to "work it and take care of it." God told Adam and Eve to be fruitful and increase in number, to fill the earth and subdue it. Life was to involve more than smelling the roses and marveling at the beauty of the orchids.[5]

From almost the first page of the Bible until the end we read about difference makers who were approved by God. Some were famous and influential; others were powerless and unknown. Some were deeply religious; others were not. A few commanded mighty armies that toppled great nations; most went about their daily activities with little apparent concern over whether their lives would make much of a difference.

Central to this biblical drama was the coming of Jesus Christ, God's Son. He lived a perfect life, taught us how to be genuine difference makers, and died to pay for the sins of people like you and me. In the lives of those who would confess their sins and make him their forgiver and leader, he promised to make a radical difference. Today he still forgives sin freely, provides abundant life on earth, and promises eternal life in heaven. Before leaving this globe, Jesus instructed his followers to be difference makers by going into all the world to make disciples.[6]

The early church sought to fulfill that mandate. Little congregations took root and grew throughout the known world. Christ's followers learned that dedicated believers would be given power, wisdom, opportunities, and special spiritual gifts that could strengthen the church and equip God's people to be difference makers.[7]

Sincere believers often differ in their interpretations of Scripture, but they agree that God, who is the sovereign and ultimate difference maker, expects us to be difference makers as well.[8]

Forgotten Difference Makers

For 50 years, long before steam engines or jet planes, John Wesley walked or rode on horseback for an estimated

225,000 miles. He preached more than 40,000 sermons and although there were no microphones, he sometimes addressed crowds larger than 20,000. He wrote no theology books and founded no evangelistic organization, but he stimulated his followers to form small groups for Bible study, prayer, discipline, support, and accountability. He developed a method for discipling others and he sent out teams of itinerant preachers. Wesley loved the poor and combined a warm-hearted evangelism with active social reform.[9] In his spare time he published an English dictionary and wrote a home medical handbook that went through more than twenty editions. Today, even his critics acknowledge that Wesley was a significant difference maker.

As he traveled the dusty rural roads, the founder of Methodism must have thought at times about the raging fire that almost snuffed out his young life. He described himself as "a brand plucked from the burning" so he could be used by God.

Clearly God did use Wesley, but he also used the forgotten men who risked their lives to rescue a frightened five-year-old from the flames. The boy grew to become a significant difference maker, but this never would have happened without those brave rescuers whose names are known only to God.

They might have been farmers who worked in the fields and rarely had time to read a book. They could have been people who struggled to make ends meet, wondered about how to raise their kids, couldn't get to college, and never found much fulfillment in life. But in one significant way these rescuers were like the little five-year-old whose sermons would someday move the world.

They, too, were difference makers.

Chapter Highlights

‡ We must seek to be difference makers because our
world depends on it; our fulfillment in life depends on
it; and God expects it.

‡ Some difference makers are famous and very
influential. For most of us, however, making a difference won't be noticed by many people. But God will
notice.

What Are the Marks of a Difference Maker?

Early in this century, shortly after World War I, a little boy in San Francisco asked his parents for a violin. This was an unusual request for a four-year-old, but the parents agreed to purchase an instrument and the boy began to play.

To everyone's surprise, he played well—very well.

Three years later he gave a concert. At age eight he had a recital at the Manhattan Opera House. Two years later he played the Beethoven violin concerto with the New York Philharmonic.

The critics were impressed and the audiences loved this pudgy little prodigy in short pants whose tiny hands could pull such beautiful music from his undersized violin.

The next year he made his European debut. While the great Bruno Walter conducted the Berlin Philharmonic, the young violinist, not yet a teenager, played concertos by the three Bs: Bach, Beethoven, and Brahms.

Audiences went wild with fervent enthusiasm. Albert Einstein, physicist and amateur fiddler, rushed backstage, hugged the young boy, and exclaimed, "Now I know there is a God!"

Round-the-world tours, front-page headlines, recording contracts, and concerts with world famous orchestras led by the finest conductors all followed as the boy moved toward adulthood.

Some say his career faltered after age twenty. Music critics complain that his adult performances have never quite equaled the stunning beauty and emotional power of his teenage recordings. Even so, Sir Yehudi Menuhin is known today as one of the greatest violinists of this century. At a time when several outstanding teenage performers are traveling around the world, captivating concert-going audiences, the now elderly Menuhin is viewed as the spiritual grandfather of today's young virtuosos.

In the world of music, Yehudi Menuhin has been a difference maker.

Peak Performers

Most of us stand in awe of prodigies like Yehudi Menuhin or the young Mozart, who gave recitals on the harpsichord at age four and wrote "Twinkle Twinkle Little Star" before he was five. We marvel at the agility of medal-winning gymnasts or the death-defying feats of circus performers, who astonish audiences with dazzling displays under the big top. We heap adulation (and money) on professional athletes who have genuine skill, and we laud their abilities, at least when they win.

But few of us can relate to these people. They aren't like us. Their feats are beyond anything we dream of accomplishing.

According to Charles Garfield, however, we could all become "peak performers." When he worked as a young computer programmer on the Apollo 11 space mission, Garfield was swept into the enthusiasm of his coworkers. Most of them were unknown individuals, committed to the common task of putting the first man on the moon. As a group, they were finding a way to make a major difference in scientific history.

Neil Armstrong's first step on the moon inspired the world and launched Charles Garfield into a new career. He began to look for people who were peak performers, individuals who might never rise to stardom but whose efforts make a difference in their work, their homes, and their communities.

Garfield found these people scattered throughout society. They are in different occupations and have different interests, but all of them have goals they want to reach. They have learned to discipline themselves and to accept responsibility for their own behavior. They respect others and work well as team members. They face as many obstacles as the rest of us and they go through rough times, but when they fail, they rarely stop for long. "No matter how rough it gets, no matter how great the assault on mind and body, peak performers always feel they can do something," Garfield observed. "Invariably, they move on."[1]

Invariably, they make a difference.

People God Uses

Like many peak performers, most of the people who made a difference in the Bible were not well known. A few had outstanding characteristics, some achieved wealth and prominence, but most did not appear qualified for the work God had given them.

Some Resisted. When he stood in the wilderness in front of the burning bush, Moses must have been glad to learn that God was about to rescue the oppressed Israelites from their Egyptian captives. But when God said, "I am sending you to Pharaoh to bring my people the Israelites out of Egypt," Moses started making excuses. The man many people consider to be Israel's greatest leader tried to get out of being a difference maker.

Jonah did something similar. He didn't resist verbally. Instead he ran away, hoping that God wouldn't notice.

Gideon was more cooperative, but twice he asked for a sign to be sure that he really was the man God wanted to lead an army into battle. When Gideon finally marched off

to war, the Lord announced that there were too many
soldiers. The army was reduced by ninety percent and only
three hundred men moved into battle. Surely some of those
men must have dragged their feet as they advanced. But
they won decisively because God was with them.[2]

Some were unqualified. Naaman was commander of the king
of Aram's army. The Bible describes him as "a great man in
the sight of his master and highly regarded." He was a
highly successful and valiant soldier. But Naaman had
leprosy.

Perhaps you remember the story of Naaman's trip to the
king of Israel, hoping to find a cure. The commander took a
fortune in gold and other treasure to pay for being healed of
his dreaded disease. When the king sent him to Elijah,
Naaman expected to be received with great honor and
healed in some dramatic way. Instead, Elijah sent a
messenger who told Naaman to wash seven times in the
dirty Jordan river. The mighty leader balked. His pride was
hurt, but his staff members persuaded him to take seven
dips in the Jordan. Namaan was cured.

Who started this whole process? We don't know her
name. She had been taken captive as a young girl from Israel
and was working as a servant for Naaman's wife. God used
this unlikely individual to suggest that Naaman could be
healed.[3]

Paul the apostle is much better known than the servant
girl. He carried the Gospel throughout the Roman Empire.
He preached frequently, but there is evidence that he was
not a good speaker. Sometimes he felt weak and even
trembled.[4] As a speaker, he didn't always know when to
quit.

Once Paul kept preaching until midnight, and one
member of the congregation, a young man named Eutychus,
dozed off. Unfortunately for Eutychus, he was sitting on the

ledge of a third-floor window. As Paul talked on, the young man toppled to the ground. Everyone thought he was dead.

"Don't be alarmed," Paul said as he stopped his sermon, went into the street, and revived the young man. Then instead of calling it quits, the apostle went back to his pulpit, picked up where he had left off, and talked on until daybreak.[5]

I don't want to be too critical of Paul. He may have been a little insensitive as a preacher, but his listeners were eager to learn. Paul clearly made dramatic changes in his world, even though he felt inadequate.

Peter was also a difference maker, but in his early life he was impulsive. Rahab was used by God even though she had worked as a prostitute. Elizabeth was a childless old lady who became the mother of John the Baptist. Mary was a simple peasant girl who pleased God and became the mother of the Messiah.

David was such a great difference maker that he is mentioned more often than any other person in the Bible. But he started life as a shepherd boy, so unqualified that his father forgot to mention him when Samuel came looking for someone to be the king of Israel.

God doesn't always use people who are wise, influential, or of noble birth to do his work. Instead, "God chose the foolish things of the world to shame the wise; God chose the weak things of the world to shame the strong. He chose the lowly things of this world and the despised things—and the things that are not—to nullify the things that are."[6] He has often selected the unlikely people of this world to be his special difference makers.

Some got off to a slow start. Abraham became a father when he was one hundred, not much older than his child-bearing wife. Moses spent eighty years in the wilderness before he emerged as the leader of Israel. Joshua was probably the oldest man in the camp when he took over and led the Israelites across the Jordan into the Promised Land.

More poignant is the story of Joseph, his father's favorite son, who was sold into slavery by jealous older brothers. Taken to Egypt by a passing caravan of merchants, Joseph was sold to Potiphar, one of Pharaoh's officials.

Joseph was well-built and so handsome that Potiphar's wife tried to seduce him. He resisted, so the spurned wife lied about the incident and her husband threw Joseph into prison. Several years passed before he was released, but in time Joseph rose to become second-in-command to the king of Egypt. Only then was he united with his elderly father and older brothers.

When Joseph's father died, his brothers knew that he could take revenge on them, but he didn't. "You intended to harm me," he explained to them, "but God intended it for good to accomplish what is now being done, the saving of many lives."[7] Joseph understood that sometimes God waits a while or puts us aside temporarily before using us to bring change. Later, he uses our experiences to make us better difference makers.

Some got off to a wrong start. God told Jonah to go to Nineveh, but he went in the opposite direction and ended up in the belly of a fish. So God gave Jonah a second chance.

Samson was a man of incredible strength whose godly service was interrupted when he fell in love with Delilah and lost both his eyes and his energy. But God heard Samson's final prayer, gave him another chance, and allowed him to push down a heathen temple filled with three thousand pagan worshipers.

David had fought a number of battles and was finally king when he slid into bed with Bathsheba one night and got her pregnant. In an attempt to cover up his immorality, David—who is described elsewhere as a man after God's own heart—lied and murdered. But God gave David another chance.

Peter was chosen to be one of the apostles, but he denied Jesus three times on the eve of the Crucifixion. When he left the courtyard of the high priest, weeping bitterly, Peter probably thought that he was finished as a disciple. But Jesus offered forgiveness and gave Peter a second chance. A few weeks later, the disciple preached a powerful sermon on the day of Pentecost and became a leader in the early church.

John Mark was one of the world's earliest missionaries. He accompanied Paul and Barnabas on their first missionary journey, but part way through the trip he quit and went home. Later Paul and Barnabas parted company because of their sharp disagreement over whether John Mark should be taken on a second trip. But God gave the young man a second chance. Later even Paul agreed that Mark had become "very helpful" in the ministry.

What can we learn from these biblical examples?

Of course God works through people who are highly educated, consistently faithful, well prepared, and in important positions. But more often God uses ordinary people to be his difference makers. He uses people who initially resist, people who seem unqualified, people who get off to a slow start, even people who have blown it previously.

God uses people like us.

What About Us?

Even if you never become a peak performer can you still be a difference maker? Will the words on these pages help you to have an influence in the lives of others? Or will this book join others you have read or skimmed and then left to collect dust on the shelf while you moved on to something else—no more of a difference maker at the end than you were before you began to read?

The answers, in part, depend on you.

I am convinced, however, that anybody who has the desire can make a difference. The early believers turned their world upside down because they were empowered by the Holy Spirit and motivated to have an impact. In a similar way, Christians today can be difference makers when we admit that we are weak but are willing to be strengthened and led by the God who is all powerful.[8]

We may grow weary at times, but we can place our hope in the Lord who never grows tired and who renews our strength.[9]

We all feel inadequate sometimes, but we serve a God who is all wise, all knowing, totally compassionate, and willing to work through people who feel incompetent.

We lack wisdom more often than we care to admit and sometimes we reach impasses that leave us bewildered. But we have a God who gives wisdom and guidance, who expects us to make plans but who then opens doors and guides our steps.[10]

Some writers or public speakers give rules and suggestions for becoming a difference maker (there are many in this book), but to have a lasting impact we need something more basic than a formula. We need to change on the inside so we develop some core difference-maker characteristics. Even that cannot be done alone. Real internal transformation is done by God, who sometimes works through other people and who seems to work more slowly than our impatient minds would like.

Sometimes the inner transformation is hindered by painful memories, past hurts, internal conflicts, or deeply hidden insecurities that we don't want to uncover and face. Problem centered self-help books might help you clear away some of these obstacles; a competent counselor is likely to do the job more effectively. It is then that we can best develop the inner traits of effective difference makers.

These traits are not impossible goals that only brilliant or exceptionally talented people can attain. These are characteristics that all of us can develop, with the encouragement of one another and with the continuing help of God.

What Kind of Difference Do We Want to Make?

The characteristics we choose to develop will determine the kind of difference we make in our world. In the familiar parable of the prodigal son,[11] we see the story of three men, each of whom made a difference because of the choices they made.

The younger brother was brash and self-centered. Instead of working at the family business, he asked for his part of the inheritance long before his father died. The father agreed, and the boy took off to see the world.

He didn't take long to spend the money. According to the Bible, "the younger son got together all he had, set off for a distant country and there squandered his wealth in wild living." Word about his lifestyle must have reached home because the family knew that much of the money had gone to prostitutes.[12]

When the funds dried up, so did the younger son's supply of friends. Alone, hungry, and in need, the boy looked for work but could only find a job feeding pigs in the fields. To make matters worse, the animals ate better than their keeper.

The prodigal son was a deplorable kind of difference maker whose life made an impact only by destroying himself and others. He didn't accomplish anything worthwhile by his wild partying, and he may have spread venereal disease through his promiscuous behavior. Back home he caused great anguish in the heart of his saddened father. All of this resulted from a young man's self-serving, self-destructive actions.

Only one good thing can be said about the Prodigal Son. He changed.

In the meantime, his older brother was back at the family ranch, plodding along every day doing his job. Maybe he was in charge of the business, making a difference by earning enough profit to pay the servants, buy food, and provide a lifestyle that enabled the father to host a big celebration with little prior planning. But the older brother felt his efforts were taken for granted. There may have been few words of appreciation or affirmation, and there was little opportunity for him to get together with friends. Unlike the younger brother, the older son was a faithful and plodding difference maker who almost got sidetracked by his angry, envious attitudes.

The father, in contrast, was a man who showed sensitivity and understanding. He was a risk taker who believed in people. How else can we explain his willingness to give the younger boy an early share of the inheritance? The father was generous, patient, compassionate, forgiving, and concerned about his children. He held a celebration when the Prodigal Son returned, but when the father heard about his elder son's reaction he left the feast immediately. He went to the fields to talk with the boy, gently urging him to be more accepting and less vindictive. The father was a difference maker because of the traits that his life reflected.

To make positive changes in our world, we must avoid sour attitudes like those that gripped the older brother, and we need to steer clear of self-destructive behaviors like those that almost ruined the Prodigal Son. We need to develop characteristics like those that we see in the forgiving father.

Chapter Highlights

‡ Some difference makers begin life as child prodigies; most of us do not.

‡ Some difference makers learn to be peak performers; but not everybody.

‡ The Bible can teach us about effective difference makers. A few had outstanding characteristics, money, and prominence, but most did not. God used difference makers who sometimes resisted, seemed unqualified, got off to a slow start, and even failed initially.

‡ You can be a difference maker, even if you grow weary at times, feel inadequate, or lack wisdom.

‡ God helps us to change so we can develop difference-maker traits.

3

What Hinders a Difference Maker?

Captain Timothy Lancaster was at the controls as the aircraft rose slowly over the rolling green hills of southern England and headed in the direction of Málaga. Strapped in their neat rows of seats, many of the passengers on that airliner were eagerly looking forward to relaxing vacations in the warm sun of the Spanish riviera.

But their journey was interrupted.

Silently and without warning, the left windshield in the cockpit popped out. The cabin quickly lost air pressure, oxygen masks dropped from their hiding places above the seats, and Captain Lancaster was pulled out of his loosened seat belt and sucked through the open window. Without hesitation, a member of the cockpit crew grabbed one of the captain's feet—and hung on. An alert cabin attendant dashed to the cockpit, strapped himself tightly into the captain's chair, and firmly grasped the other foot. The co-pilot took over the controls and headed the plane toward the nearest airport.

As the giant airliner inched gently toward the ground, each minute seemed like an eternity to the fully-conscious pilot dangling over the nose of the aircraft. Meanwhile, shocked passengers sat helplessly in their seats, unable to see the drama unfolding a few yards in front of them.

Next morning, newspapers around the world carried pictures of the pilot sitting in the hospital between his two rescuers, telling reporters that he felt fine and was ready to go back to work. The crew members who saved Timothy

Lancaster's life were difference makers who acted instinctively and with great courage.

Personal Difference Makers

Few of us have had a dramatic experience like Captain Lancaster's rescue, but we have all been influenced by others in less sensational ways. The greatest difference maker in your life may have been a teacher, pastor, high school friend, neighbor, or one of your parents. Perhaps you were influenced by an author you never met, a distant political leader, a sports figure, or a stranger who helped in a time of crisis and then disappeared.

Each of our lives has been touched by hundreds of people. Some we appreciate and respect. Others have caused immeasurable pain and turmoil, leaving us to struggle alone with bitterness and hatred. Some lives have been molded by one outstanding person, while others have been affected by so many that no one individual stands out.

There are also those among us who have struggled through life largely on their own. These people—some may be your neighbors or colleagues at work—can't think of anyone who has touched their lives deeply. They have no personal heroes and have never seen a living example of authentic Christianity.

Warren Bennis, an expert on leadership in the corporate world, believes that Americans no longer have any real heros or outstanding leaders. Once we admired Lindbergh, DiMaggio, or Astaire because they were examples of excellence; now our heroes are merely the rich and famous who have power, prestige, and lavish lifestyles.[1] In the absence of anything better, we dote on show business stars, idolize corporate kings, and even admire people who have broken the law, slipped into immorality, or dropped out of society. We prefer to read about Madonna rather than Mother Teresa because the nun leaves us feeling shallow and sinful, while the superstar leaves us feeling self-righteous and morally superior.[2]

A recent newspaper article told about a young aerospace executive who left his family and walked away from the fast-paced corporate world where he felt trapped. "Never become too good at something you hate," he told a coworker shortly before leaving. "They'll make you do it for the rest of your life."

One day he simply disappeared. For the next seven years he wandered the beaches of California as a vagabond.

Back home, his abandoned family was devastated, but at the office, his former coworkers began throwing parties on the anniversary of his departure. To them, he was a hero who had the courage to walk away from a life that he didn't like.

Real heroes and effective difference makers don't walk away from life. Instead they confront it, with all its terrors and ambiguities, and make positive changes. This is never an easy task, but some attitudes and lifestyle choices make it even harder.

Seven Obstacles to Difference Making

1. Enthusiasm without knowledge. I have a friend who bursts with enthusiasm. I've never seen him depressed, and he continually exudes gusto and vitality. Sometimes his eagerness is a little wearing, but my friend manages to inspire and motivate almost everyone he meets.

Perhaps Titus was like this. He went to Corinth "with much enthusiasm and on his own initiative." He was Paul's partner in proclaiming the Gospel and shared Paul's concern for the Corinthian believers. They in turn were eager to be helpful in providing for the relief of the church in Jerusalem. Their enthusiasm stirred other groups of believers to take similar action.[3]

Some people are enthusiastic and effervescent by nature.

This is part of their personality. Others are innately more reserved, but at times they too can be "fired up" and aroused to excitement or action.

Zeal and spiritual fervor are admirable qualities,[4] but sometimes it isn't easy to be enthusiastic and occasionally it isn't right. Even people who are naturally enthusiastic have trouble radiating zest or excitement in times of depression or boredom. And surely it is wrong and potentially harmful to be enthusiastic when our zeal is not combined with knowledge.[5]

Enthusiasm without knowledge can lead to disaster. Think of the novice seaman who enthusiastically takes his new sailboat into the open ocean without knowing how to navigate or handle his vessel. Consider the enthusiastic investor who puts money into the stock market without any understanding of the basic principles of investing. Can you imagine the danger of an enthusiastic motorcycle rider who has no idea how to control the machine or make it stop? Even those who are committed to Christ can fall into theological error and face disastrous consequences in their spiritual lives when their enthusiastic actions are not based on solid, biblical knowledge.

Difference makers often are enthusiastic, but they can hurt themselves and those they intend to help if they launch into new adventures without first evaluating the facts and thinking before they take action.

2. Ambition without capability. I'm not sure where I got the idea that it's good to be ambitious. Probably we all heard that message as kids in school, and certainly it was hammered home when I got to college. During my years in the navy I learned the importance of promotions. After graduate school I started to aggressively pursue my career— like everybody else.

Along the way I have struggled with my runaway enthusiasm. If I'm not careful, I can get caught up in time-

consuming activities, ambitious projects, and creative planning sessions with exuberant friends. Quickly my calendar
and "to do" list fill up, and I feel, at times, like I'm on a
treadmill, running to keep up with all my activities and
commitments. It doesn't help to realize that many people
feel the same way.[6]

In our competitive culture, ambition is highly prized.
We urge our kids to "get ahead." Publishers produce stacks
of books that tell us how to reach the top. A thriving
seminar business takes in millions of dollars teaching people
how to scale the corporate ladder. Even the church gets into
the act. We compete (sometimes openly but more often
covertly) for the biggest Sunday schools, the most conver-
sions, and the greatest church growth. Too often these
activities keep us so busy that we give little thought to the
spiritual condition of the people who fill our pews and
rosters.

According to the well known Peter Principle, people are
promoted (or elected) until they exceed their own levels of
competence. Blind ambition and a drive for power or
prestige make many people manipulate circumstances so
they will be offered promotions. These people find themselves with powerful opportunities, but they fail to make a
significant difference. Along the way, personal goals have
become fuzzy, consciences have become dull, motives have
become distorted, and job performance has become ineffective. Unwise decisions, inefficiency, uncontrolled spending,
gnawing fears of failure, and even lawbreaking or immorality can follow.

Incapable leaders, like fading rock stars or tired politicians, often try to deny their incompetence and protect one
another—especially from outside critics. Eventually mutual
mistrust takes root and begins to grow. Then these
incompetent individuals try to protect themselves from
their closest associates. Everyone becomes fearful of criti-

cism, losing power, or forfeiting a job to someone who is smarter, younger, or more competent. Gossip, rumor-spreading, backbiting, and efforts to defend vanishing personal turf eat up more and more of the leader's time. As the level of paranoid activity increases, work quality goes down and the ineffective leader becomes even more incompetent.

Eventually there is a fall, and the mighty topple from their pedestals.

This happens in the corporate and entertainment worlds, in academia, in the military, in government, and in the church. Often heroes fall because they have ignored a basic but unpopular biblical principle: Humble yourselves before the Lord, and he will lift you up.[7]

Jesus said something similar when he talked about servants: "Whoever exalts himself will be humbled, and whoever humbles himself will be exalted."[8]

I know a man who wants to be *the* leader in his field, but his pushy, insensitive drive for the top is alienating many people along the way. Someday he might reach his goal, but his influence will be greatly reduced because nobody will respect him.

The best and most effective leaders never set out to lead anyone, according to Warren Bennis. They have no interest in proving themselves, but they have an abiding interest in expressing themselves as freely and fully as possible. From the ranks of these people, true leaders and real difference makers emerge.[9]

Effective difference makers do not reach their positions of influence through driving ambition. They focus instead on developing competence and expertise. They concentrate on what they do best and don't waste energy on trying to maintain an artificial image of competence.

To be an effective difference maker, strive to increase

your capabilities and ask God to give you the right perspective on ambition, promotions, and upward mobility.

3. Dreaming without follow-through. My friend Wes is one of the most creative and visionary people I know. As a committed Christian, he desires to serve God effectively. His life is filled with plans and dreams about significant things that he hopes to accomplish. He is a perpetual possibility thinker.

But so far, Wes hasn't accomplished much. He can arouse enthusiasm and inspire others with his plans and ideas. I suspect he has raised a lot of money for some of his schemes, and he probably hasn't kept a cent for himself. His enthusiasm is mixed with hard work. He is careful to get the facts before he moves ahead with his plans. He is ambitious but shows humility and a sensitivity to people. His projects do not seem to be based on selfish ambition, and he has no tendency to build a personal empire. So why have his dreams never been fulfilled?

There are at least three answers.

First, Wes makes big plans but doesn't concentrate on defining and implementing the smaller steps that are necessary to reach these goals.

Not long ago I met a freshman student who asked what it would take to become a professor of psychology. "Finish your freshman year first," I replied. Then I listed some steps she would have to take to get her bachelors, masters, and doctoral degrees; to get the necessary practical experience; and eventually to get a university job. For this young lady the goal of being a professor is far away, but it can be reached (and probably will be) by moving one step at a time. People with mountaintop visions have to climb slowly if they are to reach their goals.

Second, my friend has failed to understand his own strengths and weaknesses. Wes tries to do everything himself. He fails to realize that few among us, visionaries included, have all the practical skills needed to make a big difference.

Several years ago I decided to develop and present some seminars. In preparation for the programs, I talked with people who had been very successful in the seminar business. In the end, however, my brief speaking venture bombed. The problem was not with my presentations; they were well received.

The problem was that I don't know much about marketing, advertising, book distribution, or financing seminars. I now realize that my efforts are more effective when I rely on others for advice in areas where I lack competence and expertise.

When Jesus ascended into heaven following the resurrection, he left his work in the hands of people who had varied gifts and responsibilities. He never selected one person to do everything alone. The early church understood the importance of both individual gifts and team effort.[10] Clearly, we accomplish most when we get advice and counsel from others.[11] Try to do everything yourself, and you are less likely to be an effective difference maker.

Third, Wes's visions never materialized because he selected poor associates. When he learned that he couldn't do everything alone, he joined with some colleagues and even established a board of directors.

Sadly, he didn't choose wisely. Some of his partners stole ideas from him. One dishonest business partner whom he had trusted cheated Wes out of a sizable sum of money. Wes did not understand that it takes time to check out potential partners, especially those who keep their real motives and personalities hidden.

Christians must ask God for wisdom and discernment when we want to team up with others. We must learn to watch potential partners carefully. What do others think about them? How do they conduct their business dealings?

How do they treat people, including their families? We must pay special attention to the content and impact of their spiritual lives. With these kinds of decisions it is better to hesitate and be sure, than to act too soon and be sorry.

If you want to be a difference maker it is helpful to have goals and dreams, however you must also learn to plan your steps carefully, work cooperatively with other people, and be cautious in choosing close friends and business associates.

4. Work without quality. My film career began with great promise and ended with an embarrassing fizzle.

I was invited to make a series of films to be shown in churches across the country. Soon I was working diligently preparing scripts. I traveled to California, where I met regularly with the production crew and presented my material before the camera.

When the final product appeared I was horrified. I wasn't ashamed of what I had said in those films, but their quality was terrible. Several years passed before I discovered why.

The film producer apparently was in debt when he thought of a creative way to pay his bills and earn additional money. He persuaded several investors to provide funds for a "sure-to-be-successful new film series." When the checks came in, the producer paid off his past bills and used what was left to produce the films.

The left-over money was limited and the film budget was tight. He couldn't afford top quality cameras and recording equipment, had to settle for inexpensive locations for filming, and couldn't hire a large enough production staff. Most of the work was done by two very capable but badly overworked people.

In addition, the producer had promised his investors that the films would be done quickly, so there was little time for retakes when a scene was not right the first time. Editing had to be done hastily. Everybody was under pressure and as tensions built, efficiency slid. In the rush to finish the project, quality was sacrificed and a poor product emerged.

When it was all over, the producer didn't make any profit, the investors lost money, and several people (including me) never got paid. A project that could have made a difference in many lives was scuttled.

Maybe you have had similar experiences. Try to do a project quickly, and quality always suffers. I've seen this in the publishing business when books are rushed to the presses, in schools where programs are developed without sufficient study, and in Christian ministries when new fund-raising schemes are dreamed up overnight. It is sobering to think how many sermons, political speeches, and classroom lectures have failed to have an impact because they were hastily prepared and poorly presented. The old cliché is right: Haste makes waste.

Philip Crosby knows about the importance of quality. He has been called the "elder statesman of quality management" and the "leader of America's quality revolution." For many years he has argued that a lot of money is lost when things are not done properly. Manufacturing companies spend 25 percent and more of their revenues on repairs, replacements, excess inventory, and overtime salaries for people trying to fix things that have gone wrong. Service industries incur about half their operating costs from making things right with their customers.[12]

By taking the time to do things correctly at the beginning, we can save energy, time, and money. When we strive for quality, we become more effective as difference makers. This is of special importance if we want to be difference makers for God.

The idea of quality appears in the first chapter of the Bible and is visible as an important theme throughout the pages that follow. God's ways and works are perfect.[13] When he created the world, he saw that his work was good.[14] He has no use for laziness, sloppy work, hasty actions, thoughtlessly spoken words, or eager schemes to get rich.[15] We are told, instead, that "whatever you do, work at it with all your heart, as working for the Lord, not for men. . . . It is the Lord Christ you are serving."[16] That kind of service demands care, diligence, and quality.

5. *Spending without money.* Do you have a home equity loan? If you own a house, there probably are neighborhood banks ready to give you a line of credit that will let you write a loan for yourself whenever you need a little extra cash.

When I talked to our local banker about this, he made an interesting prediction. If they aren't careful, he said, a lot of people will write checks against their equity accounts and go so far into debt that they will lose their homes.

We can understand the banker's concern. It is easy to justify writing checks for college tuition or for other needed expenses, but it is equally easy to write checks for home improvements that aren't needed or for expensive vacation packages. It is even easier to amass huge debts with credit cards. When this happens, we find ourselves paying excessive rates of interest and making payments that hardly make a dent in the total amount that we owe. If a time comes when we really need a line of credit, there may be little or nothing left.

Academic institutions, churches, businesses, parachurch organizations, and governments can all become mired in debt. They borrow with every intention of paying back the loan quickly, but unforeseen financial problems make this impossible. A business does less well than expected. Bad weather devastates a potentially lucrative crop. A hurricane or earthquake causes a slump in the tourist business. A prominent television evangelist falls into sin and contributions drop dramatically to almost every Christian institution in the country. There is no money to pay the mounting bills or interest on the loan.

Money problems can cripple difference makers.

Reaching out to others is nearly impossible when we are worried about money or immobilized by strangling financial obligations. Effective difference makers avoid the stranglehold of debt. They try to make Romans 13:8 a guiding principle for their financial lives: Owe nothing to anyone. They know that love of money and possessions can entrap us and lead to financial ruin, personal grief, spiritual disintegration, and all kinds of evil.[17]

6. *Living without growth.* When I was teaching full time, a class used to meet once a week in our home. The students would appear after dinner, usually around seven. Fresh coffee and a dessert, sometimes still warm from the oven, would be waiting in the kitchen. There would be time for small talk and laughter before we all went into the dining room and arranged ourselves around the table.

These classes were never large, in part because we had a small dining room. Sometimes I jokingly accused the students of coming for the food more than for the class, but our discussions were almost always interesting. The topics differed from week to week but the goal was always the same: to withdraw from the campus environment and think about contemporary issues that we rarely had time to discuss in the classroom. Those evening conversations were among the most challenging events of my teaching career. They kept my mind fresh and growing.

One night we turned to a book about the way people think in America. The author, a New York University professor, argued convincingly that people today don't think much at all. They prefer to be entertained. Whatever the topic, it must be presented to amuse and captivate, whether or not it informs. Even books like this one fail disastrously if the author doesn't tell enough stories to hold people's attention.

My dining room class agreed that much of this need to

be entertained comes because of television. News is presented with eye-catching pictures, bite-sized paragraphs, and short quotations—many of which are dramatic and taken out of context. Political campaigns revolve around television images of the candidates. Substantive issues are usually ignored.

Most disturbing is the effect of this entertainment mentality on the church. To keep an audience, religious programs have to entertain and give viewers what they want to see and hear. But Jesus didn't give people what they wanted to hear. He told them what they needed. He challenged their thinking and he called for change. Television, however, is not well suited for disturbing and challenging messages. "As a consequence, what is preached on television is not anything like the Sermon on the Mount. Religious programs are filled with good cheer. They celebrate affluence. Their featured players become celebrities. Though their messages are trivial, the shows have high ratings, or rather, *because* their messages are trivial, the shows have high ratings. . . . Christianity is a demanding and serious religion. When it is delivered as easy and amusing, it is another kind of religion altogether."[18]

"There's an easy solution to that problem," one of my students suggested. "Forget the tube and don't present religion on TV."

But most of us have been raised on television. It is part of our culture and it can't be ignored. An estimated ninety million Americans watch television every night. After being entertained all week and lulled into superficial thinking by short-term news clips and prime-time spectaculars, who wants to go to a boring church service—especially if it isn't entertaining? Who wants to hear somebody talk for half an hour, or longer, especially if the speech occasionally urges us to change our behavior or to use our brains? No way!

Whoever invented the term *couch potato* certainly knew

this culture. For many people, life away from their jobs involves sitting in front of a never-darkened television screen and doing nothing—like potatoes in a sack.

I have a friend like this. He's a pleasant person who probably hasn't read a book for years. In talking with him you quickly discover that he has strong and unbending opinions on almost every subject. Much of his thinking is superficial, and he sees no need to change. Every night he continues to sit in front of the tube, and his life doesn't have much impact on anyone.

Many years ago Elton Trueblood wrote that vital Christianity has three pillars: an inner life of devotion, an outer life of service, and an intellectual life of clear, rational thinking.[19] We stop growing and slip into mental and spiritual flabbiness when we ignore our devotional lives, avoid serving, or stop thinking.

Every year, usually in November, I take an hour to pull dead plants from my frost-ruined garden. The old vines that bore tomatoes or the stems that supported flowers are no longer useful for anything.

The Old Testament prophecy of Ezekiel spoke about worthless vines and so did Jesus.[20] Believers, he said, are like fruit-bearing vines. When we stay in consistent contact with Christ, determined to understand his words and to obey his commands, then we grow and are useful. Apart from him, however, we can do nothing of ultimate value. We may be living, but we aren't growing.

Difference makers keep growing. They read, keep their minds alert, and try to be open to new experiences and fresh ideas. Couch potatoes aren't very useful as difference makers.

7. *Christianity without depth.* Not long ago, I was seated on an airplane near two men who were talking about their churches. The conversation was loud and impossible for me

to ignore—although I must confess that I had an interest in what they were saying.

Apparently the men were pastors with large congregations. Their words were all very cordial, but they appeared to be playing a competitive game. Each was trying to impress the other with casual comments about the size of their services, the impact of their ministries, and the growth of their budgets.

As the conversation continued to drift in the direction of my seat, I tried not to be judgmental. Who among us does not get carried away by our excitement about work? The speakers were talking shop, like we all do, and probably they were sincere in wanting to serve Christ. Building their churches was important to them, and that is admirable. They were not men who had relegated their religious commitment to an obscure part of life.

But I wondered as they talked, if these men were too busy with their churches and their religious duties. Had they unintentionally moved away from walking with Christ, knowing him better, experiencing his power in their lives, and devoting their energies to developing spiritual depth in the members of their flocks?

Busyness, including busyness with religion and church activities, has been called "the archenemy of spiritual maturity."[21] Busy lives have little time for reflection. Never-ending waves of activity keep us from thinking carefully about the important issues in our lives—God, relationships, life purpose, goals, service. Busyness can destroy our relationships. It can stifle spiritual growth and keep us from becoming effective difference makers.

I have a very tall and agile friend who recently was invited to a three-day conference for potential players in the National Basketball Association. Fewer than one hundred athletes had been invited to attend, and everyone knew that scouts from the major NBA teams would be in attendance, looking for prospective players. The conference was to be held in a sports center not far from where we live, so my friend came a little early and stayed in our home.

But he didn't sit around. At his request, we found a vacant church gym where, for several hours, he ran up and down the floor, shooting baskets and practicing for his NBA tryout. He wanted to be ready for any unexpected hurdles that might come during this important opportunity. Constant practice, he believed, would sharpen his skills and give him greater ability to respond instinctively and immediately to any challenge on the basketball court.

Anybody who is young, tall, and in good physical condition might look like a basketball player, but NBA quality athletes need more. They need agility, intelligence, and ball-handling skills. They have to practice consistently and keep in top shape. Basketball must be a central part of their lives and thinking. Physical height and appearance aren't enough to turn anybody into a mature basketball player.

The same is true with Christians. Being in church every Sunday, carrying a big Bible, and looking like a Christian aren't enough to turn anybody into a mature believer. People who are sincere about their commitment to Jesus Christ need to keep in top shape spiritually. Knowing Christ better and determining to please him must become a central part of our lives and thinking. To keep us ready for any challenge or difference-maker opportunities, we need to develop a lifestyle that includes consistent times for prayer, Bible study, private praise, and corporate worship. We need other believers with whom we can pray and to whom we can be accountable. Religion that is squeezed into an hour or two on Sunday is superficial religion, lacking in depth and power.

In his wisdom, God often uses ordinary, sinful, even incompetent and stubborn people to be difference makers.

He doesn't wait to use us until we reach some impossibly high level of piety and spirituality. But think how much more effective and useful you could be if you became a willing, obedient player on God's team of difference makers.

Christian difference makers want to be used by God. They take their faith seriously and seek to grow spiritually. For them, knowing Christ intimately and spending time with him consistently is serious business. This is what makes potential difference makers fit for the Master's use.

Deteriorating Difference Makers

At a meeting of financial analysts, corporation president Max DePree was asked an important question: "What is one of the most difficult things that you personally need to work on?"

"The interception of entropy," the executive answered immediately.

"I'm using the word *entropy* in a loose way," the man went on to explain. "Technically it has to do with the second law of thermodynamics. From a corporate management point of view, I choose to define it as meaning that everything has a tendency to deteriorate. One of the most important things leaders need to learn is to recognize the signals of impending deterioration." Mr. DePree then listed almost two dozen "signs of entropy" that would indicate to him that his company was beginning to deteriorate.[22]

After reading this, I pulled out a piece of paper and started listing signs of entropy that could interfere, not with some giant corporation, but with my life. I will be slipping, I decided, if ever I:

‡ Stop trying to keep my class lectures interesting and start relying, instead, on dog-eared notes;

‡ Have no time to read;

‡ Try to dash off a book too quickly;

‡ Am no longer excited about my work;

‡ Don't bother to get any exercise;

‡ Get more concerned about making money than about making a difference;

‡ Stop traveling;

‡ Get carried away with ambition and forget my real goals in life;

‡ Lose interest in helping younger people grow in their spiritual lives and get started in their careers and marriages;

‡ Quit keeping a journal and stop writing out a prayer at least four or five times each week;

‡ Lose interest in growing and learning;

‡ Stop participating in worship services;

‡ Quit praying;

‡ Make Bible reading a low priority;

‡ Start debating with my critics instead of doing the work that I think God wants me to do;

‡ Get sidetracked into areas of ministry and work that may be good, but that pull me from my goals and areas of expertise;

‡ Stop planning for the future; or

‡ Spend a lot of time thinking about whether or not I will leave a legacy after I am dead.

What kind of a list would you write for yourself?

What potential dangers could keep you from being a really effective difference maker? You might want to stop at the end of this chapter and make a list of your own.

In the parable of the prodigal son, the younger brother wasted some of his best years. His actions did a lot of harm, and there is no indication in Scripture that he made a positive difference in his world.

What about you and me? Are we closet prodigals? What attitudes, personal sins, and tendencies toward entropy do we need to sweep out of our lives so that we can become effective difference makers?

Chapter Highlights

‡ Think about the significant difference makers in your life. Their example might be helpful to you.

‡ There are at least seven obstacles that could prevent you from becoming an effective difference maker.

‡ First, there is enthusiasm that isn't based on thinking and knowledge.

‡ Second, beware of ambition that makes you try to do things beyond your capabilities. Try to be competent, not famous.

‡ Third, dream about the future, but don't spend so much time dreaming that you fail to do anything else. Choose your fellow difference makers with care.

‡ Fourth, strive for quality, even if it takes more time.

‡ Fifth, beware of spending money that you don't have. You can't be an effective difference maker if you are strangled by debt.

‡ Sixth, avoid staying in a rut; keep growing. Stay in contact with Christ, open to new ideas, and not too close to television if you want to keep able to make a difference.

‡ Seventh, take the time to add depth to your Christian life. Superficial Christians rarely make much of a difference for God.

‡ Watch for signs of entropy that could keep you from making a positive difference.

Part Two
How to Be a
Difference Maker

4

Evaluate Your Thinking

Late in the summer of 1943, a young naval officer was driving a jeep near the Marine Air Base in Tontouto. World War II was raging throughout the Pacific and there was active fighting just a few miles north in the Solomon Islands.

At the sound of sirens, the driver pulled over and watched as two jeeps full of military police cleared the way for a motorcade. Expecting to see some high-ranking general, the young officer was genuinely surprised when the Army weapons carrier sped by. The passenger was a civilian, wearing a big floppy hat to protect herself from the blistering sun.

Eleanor Roosevelt had come into a dangerous war zone to encourage the troops. "Her visit made a great impression on all of us," the naval officer wrote years later. His name was Richard Nixon.[1]

President Roosevelt's wife traveled many miles to bolster morale, but more often difference makers stay at home, making an impact on their own neighborhoods.

When *Modern Maturity* magazine was looking for "people who make a difference day in, day out," a surprising group of everyday heroes emerged.[2]

Grant Cushinberry, for example, operates God's Little Half-Acre in Topeka. He gives away clothes, furniture, food, and other necessities to people in need. Every year he organizes Thanksgiving dinners for the homeless; last year there were eight thousand guests. "When it's a labor of love, it doesn't feel like work," he told a reporter.

In Philadelphia, Morris Kalmus helps young men finish

their educations and get jobs after they return from the Job Corps program. So far he has given guidance to over five hundred young people.

Across the country in Sacramento, Barbara Wiedner is founder of an organization that has attracted attention from the Gorbachevs and Barbara Bush. Mrs. Wiedner had never been involved in political activities until she learned that a nearby air base was stockpiling nuclear weapons. Concerned about future generations, the grandmother joined a group of protesters, holding a sign proclaiming herself a "grandmother for peace." Others noticed and eventually Grandmothers for Peace became an international organization.

After teaching for thirty-five years in Bremerton, Washington, Jen Southworth retired and began tutoring people who need help in reading, speaking, and writing English. She finds nothing more fulfilling than to "see the light dawn on their faces when they really understand."

All of these difference makers and others like them are active people. Each is doing something worthwhile and their actions are having an impact.

It is easy to be inspired by stories of active people who are making a difference in the lives of others. But some people, like President's wives, have more opportunities than the rest of us. Others, like the active difference makers in the magazine story, are retired and better able to control what they do with their time. Apparently these people don't have sick relatives who need constant care or jobs that always demand extra time. Perhaps their kids don't have endless needs and their lives aren't filled with mundane tasks and boring responsibilities. But the rest of us can feel frustrated by the overwhelming demands on our time.

Every Sunday morning I teach a class of young married couples who feel these pressures. Most of them are involved in building their careers, their marriages, and their families.

We study the Bible together and try to apply its teachings to our busy lives.

One morning I mentioned a conference that I had read about and suggested that the conference theme would be good for our class: "Courage to be Different—Commitment to Make a Difference."

The couples listened politely but didn't show much response. Most of them are active people, overflowing with talent and serious about their spiritual growth. Many are young professionals and some might be considered yuppies. In general, this is a responsive group, enthusiastic and bursting with potential. These people aren't afraid to be different and many are committed to making a difference. Why did they seem so unresponsive when I talked about the conference theme?

I got the answer after class. "It's a great idea," someone said. "Probably most of us do want to be different and to make a difference. But right now a lot of us are just trying to survive!"

Maybe you feel that way. You would like to make an impact for Christ, but your life is besieged by so many time gobblers that you struggle to keep up. When we are trying to survive, who's got time to be a difference maker?

I thought of this recently when I was reading in the book of Hebrews. In the eleventh chapter, we read a roll call of the Bible's greatest heroes. Most appear to have been active people. Some struggled to survive, but they still made an impact. Some saw their efforts lead to impressive results. Others were tortured to death without seeing any evidence that their lives had mattered. But these were all people of faith who knew that God had seen their dedication and would reward their endeavors in the end.

These heroes of faith were difference makers who had lived according to principles that we see in Hebrews 12 and 13. Relying on these guidelines, we will consider fourteen practical actions any of us can take to become difference makers.

Principle Number One: Get and Keep the Right Mindset

Few people like homework. Most students hate doing it, and their teachers don't like grading it. The same is true for athletic training. Winning a race or playing in a championship game might be fun, but getting in shape and developing athletic skills can be boring and difficult. Becoming part of a profession isn't any easier. Long lonely hours of study and preparation for demanding examinations have to come first. It isn't surprising that many people have big dreams but aren't willing to go through the work, study, and discipline that would make their dreams come true.

To be a difference maker you have to start where you are, surrounded by the people with whom you live and work. You have to begin with the abilities you've got and start by taking a long careful look at your thinking.

Life is like a race. The writer of Hebrews urges us to "throw off everything that hinders and the sin that so easily entangles, and let us run with perseverance the race marked out for us" (Hebrews 12:1). For most of us, this isn't a short sprint; it's a long marathon. The Christian runner who wants to reach the finish line without collapsing or dropping out needs preparation. We must get rid of all the hindrances that can trip us up.

What hinders you? Though we each would answer differently, all of us get tangled in harmful ways of thinking.

Negative Thinking

Some people have negative, self-defeating ways of thinking. They go through life crippled by ideas and memories that have been imprinted on their minds, sometimes by individuals from the past who thought the criticisms would be helpful. Many of us have heard repeatedly that we won't amount to anything, that we have no talent, that we need to shape-up, that we are too stupid or too incompetent or too clumsy to make a difference. After a while we begin to believe these messages, especially if we have had failures that make us think the messages are right. Like a compact disc that plays over and over, we keep telling ourselves that nothing will change and we give up hope of making a difference even before we start.

But God uses imperfect people to be difference makers. Imperfect people are the only kind he's got right now. It is neither easy nor wise to ignore our weaknesses, our past failures, or the opinions of others who consistently have made derogatory comments about us. But these thoughts can bog us down. They can be the Devil's hindrances and entanglements to immobilize our thinking and to keep us from running the Christian-life race with strength. If we keep believing the bad recordings that play in our minds or the negative words we hear from others, self-defeating thinking will hold us back.

Positive Thinking

Periodically, I receive a brochure or form letter telling how I can change my life if only I will change my attitude. A recent promotion piece was typical: "Our program, we can confidently say, has changed more lives and helped create more millionaires than any other program ever produced. And, because it helps people get their lives and careers on track, it has saved many marriages too."

With enthusiasm and strings of superlatives, the six-page letter promised that by purchasing and listening to a program of cassette tapes, I could move "to the very top," earn more than 95 percent of the rest of the population, and join the ranks of millionaires. "I can say without hesitation that you are smarter than you think you are," the impersonal form letter continued. By hearing the cassettes I was told that my mental capacity could double, my efficiency could increase by 50 percent, and I would make a lot more money. Most incredible—and from my perspective incredibly wrong—was the statement that "money, success, and spiritual values are all so closely linked, it is almost impossible to achieve the first two and lose the third."

Motivational speakers who give rousing speeches and write inspiring books about positive thinking seem to imply that anyone can throw aside insecurities and soar to the top. All it takes to succeed is to think positively. There are no individual differences, except differences in attitude. Each of us can achieve whatever our minds believe.

I can understand the motives of people who want to inspire and encourage others to cast off their negative thinking and to get on with the business of living. But possibility thinking can also hinder the run through life. Psychologists have demonstrated what we all know: Individuals have different abilities, strengths, capacities, and personalities. It is wrong, even cruel, to imply that some young person with low intelligence and limited funds can get through medical school armed only with a positive mental attitude. Young athletes who lack talent may overflow with positive thinking and determination, but they still won't get into the big leagues.

Proud Thinking

Late in the 1960s, when church renewal was a hot topic, Robert Girard gathered a small congregation together in Arizona. It was "an incongruous mix of pioneers, visionaries, church dropouts, ecclesiastical and emotional misfits, spiritual cripples, wounded healers, sightseers, and saints," the pastor wrote later. "Some of us were angry young dreamers on an exciting adventure. A vision of the church as it could be drove us on. . . . We loved each other. Fought and argued with each other. Yelled at each other. And hammered out consensus on some extremely difficult doctrinal issues. But we continued to love one another in the face of it."[3] Whatever their differences, the members of Our Heritage Church all wanted to be difference makers— for God.

And they were.

People from around North America began to hear about the church. Many came to observe its operation. The pastor wrote a book that sold over 100,000 copies and suddenly he was in great demand as a speaker at conferences, seminars, colleges, and seminaries. Invitations came from around the world. His book was translated into other languages and made required reading in a number of theological schools. People were coming to Christ. The church was growing. A sense of community was developing. Clearly Robert Girard and his congregation were making a difference, "on the leading edge of a spontaneous movement that looked as if it might profoundly affect the direction of the evangelical church world."

Then, as quickly as it arose, the church collapsed.

Many tried to explain why. Some thought the church had focused so much on innovation and renewal that Jesus was subtly ignored. Others noted the lack of evangelism or willingness to submit to authority. Unwise leadership decisions disrupted some of the unity. There was no willingness to hear or to heed the cautions of outside observers. Instead, a spiritual smugness permeated many of the believers. "Our way of 'doing church' became to our minds almost the only right way," Girard wrote later. "Other groups, other churches, other Christians were doing it wrong. No one else was as right as we were. No one else was as transparent, as unencumbered, as emancipated, as close to the New Testament ideal and priorities as we were. . . . The suggestion that something real might be happening elsewhere was viewed with a jaundiced eye."[4]

In pondering why his vision vanished, Robert Girard put much of the blame on himself. He was an angry man whose church had attracted other angry men and women. Insecurity, paranoia, compulsiveness, and guilt characterized his inner life. There was little depth or reality in his personal walk with God. Like all of us, he was a spiritual struggler, needy and weak, but he tried to keep this hidden. Instead, the pastor toiled to maintain the "spiritual leader image" that he knew to be a façade. In church, Girard was an ecclesiastical showman, trying to perform in the ways that people expected. Like millions of others, his ego and his self-worth were tied to his work.

When the work collapsed, so did Robert Girard.

The following years were filled with pain and turmoil. Robert Girard was a broken man: almost fifty, out of work, and feeling like a huge failure. He needed time to heal. He needed the loving support of caring people and the help of an insightful counselor. He needed to reevaluate his life and focus on his walk with God.

While this process of recovery inched forward, the former pastor took a job pumping gas and served as a volunteer fireman. He and his family moved out of town to a small community where nobody knew about Our Heritage Church. With no prior experience, he built his own house. After some time passed, he reluctantly agreed to become pastor of a little church in the nearby town of Lake Montezuma. There, a wiser and more mature Robert Girard is still making a difference.

In his great mercy, God sometimes uses us to make a difference even though we have unresolved spiritual and emotional struggles, questionable motives, and unhealthy attitudes. But the pastor and many of the people in Our

Heritage Church grew beyond these shortcomings and learned some valuable lessons about proud thinking.

They learned, for example, that *bigger is not necessarily better*. Their original church made the mistake of assuming that they were successful and making a lasting difference because their numbers were increasing and their influence was growing. They had slipped into the devastating delusion of what J. I. Packer has called "the sickness of worshiping growth more than God."

The book of Acts records statistics, but at no place in the New Testament are believers commended because of increasing attendance, expanding influence, or the prominence of a leader. Far more important are changed lives, consistent love, doctrinal purity, Christlike character, spiritual growth, and the development of believers who obey God's Word and do not deny his name.[5]

If you want to make a difference, don't spend time worrying about bigness. Instead, humble yourself before the Lord, do your work as well as you can, and assume that he will lift you up and increase your influence if that is his plan. Don't seek after big numbers and prominence, but if you become well-known, don't resist. On the other hand, remember that small and faithful difference makers are sometimes more influential than the famous and powerful. Whatever happens, we should bear in mind Paul's words to the Colossians: "Continue to live in him, rooted and built up in him, strengthened in the faith as you were taught, and overflowing with thankfulness."[6]

The people of Our Heritage Church also learned that *creativity and innovation do not necessarily bring permanent change*. This is no criticism of creative and committed people who freely yield their talents toward making a difference for Christ. Too many churches and lives are marked by perpetual dullness, stifling routines, and a rigid refusal to change. To keep from drying up, we all need freshness and innovation in our lives and times of worship.

We who admire talent and originality, however, sometimes find it hard to believe that God uses weak people, even some who are not very competent or creative. Hudson Taylor, the great missionary statesman, once suggested that "all God's giants have been weak people."

This message isn't popular, but it is true, nevertheless. As Robert Girard observed, God's most effective difference makers seem to have "gone through some type of weakening process to break the outer shell of arrogance, self-righteousness, and dependence on personal strength, charisma, and talent. God uses failure, sickness, breakdown, sin, personal tragedy, and sorrow to reduce his people to usefulness. Unless the servant of God learns to depend utterly on God and to forsake self-dependence of any kind, he or she remains too strong to be of much value."[7] This doesn't mean that we should seek to be weakened. It means, instead, that we can expect weakening if we are serious about making a difference.

The heroes of the faith listed in Hebrews 11 recognized that God worked through weakness rather than pride.[8] They were not negative thinkers, but neither were they unrealistic, hyped-up possibility thinkers. Instead, they were yielded thinkers.

Yielded Thinking

When Moses and the Israelites stood on the border of Canaan, ready to possess the Promised Land, twelve spies were sent in to have a look. All were deeply impressed with the richness and fertility of the area, but ten of the twelve were convinced that any invasion surely would fail. The inhabitants of Canaan were too big and strong.

Two of the spies, Caleb and Joshua, disagreed. "We should go up and take possession of the land, for we can certainly do it," Caleb roared with conviction in a speech before the people. "The Lord is with us. Do not be afraid of them." But the listeners responded by threatening to stone the two spies.[9]

You remember what happened next. The nation wandered in the wilderness for forty years, and only two of the original group entered the Promised Land, Caleb and Joshua. Some might argue that they had a positive mindset, and in a way they did. But their thinking was motivated by a belief that God could accomplish great things through weak people who were yielded to him.

A similar yielded mentality was seen years later when Isaiah heard the Lord's voice saying "Whom shall I send? And who will go for us?" Without hesitation, Isaiah responded: "Here am I. Send me!"[10]

When he prayed before the Crucifixion, Jesus was clearly yielded to the Father. "I have brought you glory on earth by completing the work you gave me to do," he said.[11] Throughout his brief ministry Jesus had demonstrated and emphasized the importance of whole-hearted obedience among God's people.

Most Christians want to do great things for God. Such a willing attitude surely pleases him. But he isn't pleased when we dream of possibilities and make great plans without seriously yielding to his guidance. He isn't pleased when we come to him with grandiose ideas, expecting a rubber stamp approval and divine blessing because our ideas are intended to glorify God. Sadly, these man-made plans often fail and the planners are disillusioned.[12] Their motives may be good but they miss something crucial: God wants us more than he wants our plans. He reserves major difference-making roles for people who say, "Here I am, Lord, willing and available. Show me what you want me to do."

As we develop this attitude with God's help, we are given opportunities to influence people's lives. This happened to me during an unplanned meeting with one of my students.

The campus was dark and quiet when I turned onto the road leading to my office. Rarely was I there at such a late hour, but I had been to a meeting downtown and had decided at the last minute to pick up my mail before heading home.

Absentmindedly I drove over the familiar road and almost failed to notice the lone figure that appeared briefly in the path of my headlights. He was walking slowly, both hands stuffed in his pockets, a narrow collar raised slightly to protect his neck from the cold autumn wind.

By slowing down and squinting a little, I was able to recognize the face. He was in one of my classes, an Asian student whose name I didn't know.

"What are you doing out at this hour of the night?" I asked in a cheerful voice as I rolled down the window and slowed the car to a stop. "Hop in. I'll give you a ride."

Five minutes later we were in my office, perched on opposite corners of the secretary's desk, a small stack of unopened mail between us.

"I went for a walk to do some thinking," my student said. He had needed some quiet time, away from the noisy dormitory, to ponder his career goals, his family in Japan, and his frustrations with the first few weeks of the fall semester. He radiated loneliness, fatigue, and discouragement.

"It's different here from what I expected," he said. "I'm thinking of dropping out of school for a while."

Neither of us can remember much about the conversation that followed. We chatted for about an hour before I drove him to the dorm and headed on home.

The student, a young man named Masaru Horikoshi, decided to stay in school. Because of our late night encounter on campus, we became good friends. He came to our house for dinner, got to know my family, and returned many times prior to his graduation.

He must have mentioned us in letters to the family because his father, pastor of a large church near Nagoya, knew about me when we met a year or two later in Japan. I was invited to speak at a conference and soon found myself crossing the Pacific twice a year to work with Japanese pastors in developing pastoral counseling. In the meantime, Masaru had enrolled in a doctoral program, and he and I started doing seminars together in Tokyo.

At times Masaru and I think back to that late night meeting and agree: It was not a chance encounter. God gave me the opportunity to spend a brief time encouraging a young man who was at a turning point in his career. Because of that encounter, we both have been given fresh opportunities to make at least a little difference in the lives of Japanese pastors who minister in one of this world's most advanced but stress-filled nations. The young man who walked the campus on that autumn night several years ago is emerging as someone who can make significant changes for God in Japan.

As we yield ourselves to God, we will have unexpected meetings like that. The encounters might not be dramatic. Frequently they are soon forgotten, but those conversations make long-lasting differences in many lives.

The Indirect Approach

Have you ever noticed how many things in life do not yield to a direct approach? Try to find happiness, and you probably will miss it; work on something worthwhile, and happiness will come as a by-product. Try to influence someone by pushing or cajoling, and your efforts probably will fail; live your life with integrity and love, and you will have an influence. Try to force someone to trust you and it won't work; be dependable and live in a way that is honest and trustworthy and others will give you their trust. Work to build goodness, gentleness, peace, or joy into your life, and success will be limited; live guided by the Holy Spirit while seeking to glorify God, and your inner life will change. Try to generate an ecstatic, spiritual experience, and it won't happen; spend time getting to know God better, and you will discover that great spiritual moments come unbidden, often when they are least expected.[13]

The same principle applies to making a difference. Organizations, mission agencies, and churches often overflow with plans and programs, many of which fail to accomplish much. Sometimes our carefully constructed career plans get us nowhere. Tragically, many of our lives are meaningless and unproductive despite our earnest desires to accomplish something worthwhile.

The reason for this lack of productivity lies at the very core of our being and in a basic teaching of Jesus. If you want to have an impact, be a servant.

Books and seminars on leadership often talk about taking charge, getting power, and being in control. Rarely do we encounter anything about serving.

That isn't surprising. Servanthood is such a unique Christian concept that even the disciples seemed surprised when Jesus raised the idea. They had been squabbling about their place in God's kingdom, so Jesus made a remarkable statement: "Whoever wants to become great among you must be your servant, and whoever wants to be first must be your slave." Jesus himself was their example of servant leadership.[14]

Throughout his ministry, Jesus was shadowed by Pharisees who were pompous, highly critical, and clearly threatened. These men liked to have titles, acclaim, respect, and places of honor at banquets and in the synagogues. Many of them pretended to be pious difference makers, but Jesus called them hypocrites.

Watch out for them, he told the disciples. They look holy on the outside, but inside they are full of wickedness, greed, and self-indulgence. They do not practice what they preach, and they like to be seen as great leaders, even though they are blind fools. Then Jesus repeated a message that the disciples had heard before: If you want to be great, be a servant.[15]

If you want to make a difference, make it your practice to serve others by encouraging, helping, caring, and showing love. If you want to be a Christian difference maker, first devote yourself to becoming like Jesus.

This is likely to involve preparation and careful planning. Soldiers are useless in battle if they have not trained. Undisciplined football teams will not make it to the Super Bowl. Good lawyers don't win court cases without careful preparation.

But training and preparation involve more than developing skills. To be effective in combat, a good soldier must develop a military way of thinking. Athletes must "think sports," and team members must think like winners. Professional people learn a way of thinking that permeates their lives.

The same is true of Christians. No believer will make a great difference if he or she is so busy doing things that there is little time to spend with God. We won't make much of a difference in God's kingdom if we don't make the effort to learn how he thinks and how those thoughts express themselves through servant leadership.

Two Basic Attitudes

After completing all the course work and examinations for my degree in psychology, I took my internship at a large treatment center in Oregon. I was still in my twenties when I moved to Portland and encountered a host of difference makers who profoundly affected my life.

The internship training was excellent. I found a number of new colleagues and fellow students. I got involved in a very fine church and eventually took courses in the theological seminary where I met the woman who became my wife. During those years in Oregon, she and I met some of the finest people whom we have ever known. Two of those couples greatly influenced my life.

Art and Berniece Matthews were sponsors of the church college and career group. I spent hours in their home and invited myself for dinner more often than I care to admit. They never seemed to resent those sometimes insensitive intrusions and always made me feel welcome. They showed me how to lead by serving others. When I look back, they are high on the list of difference makers who made a quiet but powerful influence in my life.

M. L. and Marilynn Custis made a difference too. M.L. was a physician who taught a young adult Bible class, spent time with me, and tried (unsuccessfully) to teach me how to play golf. This gentle doctor gave me a deeper understanding of professional ethics and showed a Christ-centered lifestyle. He and his wife served as informal premarital counselors, loaned me money for the engagement ring, and paid for our wedding cake because we couldn't afford to buy one.

In expressing our thanks, I once asked M.L. how we could ever pay him back. Julie and I have never forgotten his answer. "Probably you can't pay us back," he said. "Don't even try. Instead, go and do the same for others."

A few years later, M. L. Custis died suddenly in the prime of life. We never got to pay him back for his kindness. But we have tried to follow the doctor's advice and have shared it often with students and other people who come to our home. It is biblical advice, similar to what Jesus taught after telling the parable of the good Samaritan.[16] If someone is kind to you or if someone makes a difference in your life, do the same for others.

How were the Matthews, Dr. and Mrs. Custis, and numerous other Portlanders able to show such kindness and make such a difference in our lives? They were motivated by their commitment to Christ, but each of them also showed the two most important ingredients for making a difference. They were determined to make a difference, and they found a way.

Wanting to make a difference. Throughout his ministry, Jesus met people who wanted to become his followers until he told them what it might cost. It will be hard, like carrying a cross, he once said. Your family might reject you and you probably will have to leave home. Your critics and opponents might pull you apart like a wolf tears into a sheep. You will have to dispense with your riches, cast off your bitterness, and show forgiveness instead of revenge. Some people will hate you, and you might lose your head like John the Baptist. When they heard these descriptions, many were like the rich young ruler who turned and walked away.

Still the cost of making a difference can be high, especially if you want to be committed to Christ. You will be inconvenienced, probably many times. Your commitment may pull you away from home, eat up your time, drain your energies, and use up your money. Life will sometimes be both difficult and uncomfortable. You might have to work very hard under terrible conditions for little or no pay. There may be few words of appreciation from anyone. You may face rejection, biting and unjust criticism, and personal betrayal. You may work diligently for certain causes, only to see another get the credit. People may take you for granted and never say thanks. Despite giving your best, you may feel that your efforts are futile and your life isn't amounting to anything.

But there are great and eternal rewards. Difference

makers have an inner sense of satisfaction. Even when their efforts appear to have failed and nobody notices what they have tried to do, they know, deep inside, that they at least made the effort. It is better to have tried and failed than to reach the end of life knowing that you weren't even concerned about making a difference.

Very often, of course, difference makers see benefits from their labors: lives that have changed, projects that have been completed, goals that have been accomplished, children who have been launched into life, church ministries that have advanced, in part, because of their efforts. A few people get plaques, scrolls, medals, and citations for their efforts, but those are rare. More often we get an occasional letter or a word of appreciation, although usually we don't even get that.

But we know that God is aware of our motives and efforts. He notices and doesn't forget when we show love to him and lend a helping hand to his people.[17] He never promises success on earth, but he will give rewards in heaven.[18] He doesn't demand or expect that we all will make a significant impact on this world, but he does call us to be faithful.[19] He does not anticipate perfection while his people are on earth, but he requires us to "love the Lord your God with all your heart and with all your soul and with all your mind" and to love our neighbors even as we love ourselves.[20]

These are high standards. To become a difference maker, you must weigh the options and then decide if you really want to make the effort.

Finding a way to make a difference. When I was a graduate student, before taking that internship in Oregon, I had a classmate who was an excellent athlete. Often we would study together and pump one another with psychological questions, but Peter would always find time to go jogging or to play a little tennis. He spoke wistfully and often about his summers sailing off Cape Cod and he sometimes dreamed about becoming a sport psychologist who would work mostly with athletes.

More than once in those days before we turned thirty, my friend talked about middle-aged men who were overweight and out of shape. "That," he said firmly, "will never happen to me." I haven't seen Peter for many years, but I have wondered if he kept his resolve to keep in shape.

For many of us, controlling weight is a continual struggle. Often we want to slim down. We have the will to be in shape but doing something about this is a lot harder. It is easier to talk about reducing than to start on and stick with a diet.

Making a difference is somewhat the same. Wanting it is easier than doing it—and doing it often starts with little things: writing an overdue letter or a note of appreciation, speaking kindly to a busy waitress, taking the time to do something right, stifling the temptation to gossip, taking a friend to the airport, listening to your kids when they want to talk, encouraging some person who has a creative idea, listening to somebody's struggles even in the middle of the night.

No one person can do everything, and we shouldn't try. Even Jesus pulled away from the crowds so he could be alone, pray, and perhaps examine his priorities.[21] None of us can respond to all the appeals for money that flood our mailboxes. I can't send free books to all the people who request them. I can't talk to or counsel all the strangers who call on the telephone. Sometimes I can't even answer all my correspondence, no matter how much I want to or how hard I try.

At various times over the years I have felt swamped by the busyness of my life and frustrated because all of this activity didn't seem to be accomplishing anything. But life is sometimes like that. Washing dishes, changing diapers, mowing grass, paying bills, cleaning house, taking out the garbage—these kinds of things will be with us always. They eat into our schedules and gobble up time, but they can't be ignored.

Once you decide that you want to make a difference and you are determined to find a way, take a good look at your life. Decide how much of your busyness comes from inefficiency and jumbled priorities. To help with your evaluation, take the life status check in the appendix of this book.

Making Furniture and Making a Difference

Herman Miller, Inc., is a furniture company in Zeeland, Michigan, a place once described as "a frosty town with no bars, no pool halls, and no theaters." The Herman Miller company is small, but *Fortune* magazine ranked it as one of the hundred best companies to work for in the United States. It was ranked ninth in a survey of the most admired corporations and sixth in terms of the quality of management.

The people at Herman Miller want to make a difference. "We intend to make a contribution to society," the president wrote recently. "We wish to make that contribution through the products and services we offer, and through the manner in which we offer them. . . . We intend to be socially responsible and responsive."[22] Words like this make me want to stand on my chair and cheer.

Sometimes individual difference makers can learn from corporate leaders who are trying to make a difference through their companies. The chief executive officer of Herman Miller defines leadership as the art of liberating people to do what is required in the most effective and humane way possible. Employees are encouraged to strive for quality, not just in the furniture they manufacture, but in their service, customer relations, willingness to keep promises, and care for one another. The company is always looking for ways to improve, always seeking to help employees feel needed and important, always encouraging innovation and further education, constantly striving to equip people and empower them to do their best. The employees help make decisions and share in company profits. There is a giving of time, energy, and money to the community, not as a public relations gimmick, but because of the belief that we cannot live our lives isolated from the needs of society. The company is marked by integrity and mutual respect, and the people who work for Herman Miller make a difference.

A lot depends on their attitudes.

Maybe none of the employees has ever heard a motivational tape, but they work together and do their best because of a respect for one another, a willingness to change, a commitment to quality, and a determination to make a difference.

If you've got the right attitudes, you can make a difference too.

Chapter Highlights

‡ To be a difference maker, we have to keep the right mindset. God will help us with this, especially if we are willing to be yielded to him and obedient.

‡ Things that are bigger, more creative, and innovative are not necessarily better.

‡ Effective difference makers need a willingness to think like a servant.

‡ The best difference makers want to have an impact and they find ways to have an impact.

5

Avoid Sinful Entanglements

After his involvement with Bathsheba, David's life was a wreck. By his own admission, he felt drained, weighted down, depressed, guilty, physically exhausted, and sick. He was rejected by his friends, pursued by his enemies, unable to sleep, and unwilling to eat.[1]

But when he finally confessed his sin and asked for God's forgiveness, David's whole mental attitude changed. He began to sing, to feel a new sense of joy and hope for the future, to tackle his responsibilities with new confidence and enthusiasm, and to yield himself again to God's sovereign leading. "Show me the way I should go," he prayed. "Teach me to do your will, for you are my God; may your good Spirit lead me."[2]

In his book about Hebrews 12, Erich Sauer describes how sin trips and entangles us. In the beginning, sin comes as a generous friend, promising pleasure, progress, and possibilities for the future. When he started his work, the Devil tempted Eve with the promise of greater knowledge and prestige. "Try it; you'll like it," he said in essence. "Your eyes will be opened, and you will be like God." When the promises are enticing, it is easy to take the bait. Most often some pleasure does come and there may be no immediate feelings of remorse or entrapment.

In time, however, the sin is seen for what it really is: a devastating tyrant. Before the deed, its wickedness was minimized. Afterward its effects are magnified. That which dazzled now surrounds us with darkness. The things that promised to free us for greater pleasure and fulfillment are

79

found to bind us and lead us into depression. The Evil One, who came first masquerading as a friend, now becomes an accuser who robs us of our courage and convinces us that there is no hope that we will ever again be pure and free and useful.[3]

Principle Number Two: Keep Working to Clear Out the Sin in Your Life

This is not a popular message. We don't even like to use the word *sin*; it seems so out of date and irrelevant. But this is a crucial message if we really want to be difference makers for God.

Hebrews 12:1 instructs us to "throw off . . . the sin that so easily entangles." To be used by God, we constantly need to beware of the potential entanglements of sin. Only then can we move on to be effective difference makers.

Many of us are like a gardener who wants to produce a good crop of vegetables or a bright display of flowers but is unwilling to clear away the weeds and to turn over the dirt. Our goals may be worthy, but we won't reach them without prior spade work. For the Christian difference maker, that initial preparation involves clearing away the sin from our lives—admitting it, confessing it, and forsaking it—with the help of God.

We need to carve time out of our busy schedules to look at our lives. Be honest with yourself. What kinds of attitudes, persisting behaviors, grudges, self-indulgent choices, indiscretions, fantasies, or other evidences of disobedience are standing between you and God? Human beings are imperfect creatures, marred by the Fall, tempted by sin, and often trapped by sin as well. These things block us from becoming effective difference makers.

Such self-examinations, of course, are not one-time events. We are surrounded by temptations and sometimes we fall. When that happens, we need to get up and start over, knowing that God forgives as we confess our sins. He is always willing to give us another chance.[4]

Four Difference Maker Qualities

Getting untangled from sin is not just a matter of resisting the temptations that trip us up. When we confess our sins in a genuine attitude of repentance, God forgives freely because his son Jesus Christ has taken the punishment for what we have done. Slowly he remakes us into people whose lives are marked by growing love, joy, peace, patience, kindness, goodness, faithfulness, gentleness, and self-control. As these traits grow, so does our potential to be difference makers.[5]

These are not the only qualities that mark the lives of people who are making a difference. Warren Bennis has devoted his entire career to the study of leadership. At one time president of the University of Cincinnati, he works now as a consultant to governments and multinational companies. His books on leadership are among the most popular in the business.[6]

In one of these books, Bennis reports some interesting discoveries that came from his five-year study of people who are "leading to make a difference."[7] He discovered that true leaders have balanced lives. Their careers and their personal lives fit together harmoniously. They are ambitious and often talented, but they are not driven to reach the top or enslaved by a passion to get ahead. The best leaders know their strengths, weaknesses, capabilities, and limits. They work within these boundaries, do the best job possible, and consistently inspire others to do the same.

This sounds good coming from an author who writes to inspire potential leaders, but can it apply to people who have no leadership responsibilities or aspirations? Do conclusions about super leaders speak to those of us who simply want to be difference makers? Can any of this be applied to Christians?

Based on his research, Warren Bennis identified several basic ingredients of leadership that each of us can develop, whether or not we aspire to be leaders. These traits—we might call them the four marks of a difference maker—can be developed in all of us. Integrity, commitment, humility, and a willingness to learn will characterize true difference makers. Each has a clear biblical mandate. As we pursue them, we are less likely to get tangled up in sin.

Integrity. This involves doing what you know is right even when others aren't looking. Joseph showed integrity when he resisted the seductions of Potiphar's wife, even when he was far from home and his sexual urges may have gone unsatisfied for a long time. Daniel, who also became a great leader in a pagan nation, showed integrity when he refused to defile himself with the royal food and wine. He showed integrity when he continued to worship God openly because he knew this was right, even though he knew, too, that he would be thrown into a den of lions because of his public prayer.[8]

People of integrity can be trusted to be faithful. If they promise something, they will do it. Their actions are built on high moral principles. Their words are not spoken for gossip, spreading rumors, tearing others down, or distorting the truth. People of integrity discover what pleases God. Then they do it. Christians with integrity are committed both to hearing God's Word and to doing what it says.[9]

In recent years we have been swamped with stories about scandals among politicians, Wall Street traders, athletic heros, entertainment figures, and religious leaders. The reasons for these sinful and self-defeating behaviors are complex, but most can be traced to a basic lack of integrity. Bennis called scandals, "The sum of a million and one undiscovered, uncounted small cheatings, evasions, cover-ups, half-truths, and moral erosions not only in our alleged leaders but in the whole society."[10]

People who lack integrity often begin in little ways, with minor deviations from what they know is right. In time, these deviations become more frequent. They become a normal part of life. Integrity gradually disintegrates.

You cannot force integrity onto someone else; you can only develop and model it in your own life. Integrity is not something reserved for a few, high-visibility leaders. It needs to be at the core of all our lives. Integrity is basic to both effective leadership and effective difference making. Without integrity neither your life, your work, your family, your company, nor your church will make much of a lasting difference.

Commitment. Most of the men and women who worked on the Apollo space project were motivated by a mission. They were dedicated to a goal and excited about having a part in the upcoming lunar landing. Few had worked previously at extraordinary levels, but their capabilities and their capacities blossomed because they were buoyed by enthusiasm and lifted by a sense of purpose.

It wasn't surprising that performance went back to business-as-usual once the Apollo project ended. The efforts of the workers were no longer sustained by a passion. They had soared to the heights and slid quickly back to earth.

Life is like that. For most of us, periods of unusual excitement and emotional fervor are rare deviations from the ordinary, day-to-day activities that mark our lives. Any of us can get swept into the excitement of a championship game, an emotional worship experience, a new love, or an exhilarating project at work. But things that last are not built on temporary enthusiasm, shifting moods, or the words of a dynamic speaker. Strong marriages, great works of art, significant inventions, personal maturity, spiritual growth, stable government, lasting relationships, solid scholarship, quality manufactured products, the uprooting of corruption, excellence in education—these only come when people have intense and unwavering commitments.

A commitment is a strong, abiding belief in some thing or person. Without commitments, we float from one activity to another, from one experience to the next. Without commitments we never become peak performers and we rarely make any significant difference. A commitment is something that lasts; real commitments don't keep changing. Occasionally, of course, we commit to something and discover later that we made a mistake and have to change. To prevent too many of these shifts, we need to choose our commitments carefully and thoughtfully.

When we are committed to a person or cause, we give up some of our freedom and independence, some of our individuality and control.[11] This can be risky, and some people are never willing to relinquish control or make any commitments. Instead they drift rudderless through life, without direction or goals. These people rarely make a difference.

When my parents celebrated their golden anniversary, the family held a reception so friends could come to offer congratulations. Several guests commented that it was remarkable and unusual for two people to stick with each other for half a century. How did they do it?

My mother and father had rough times in their marriage, but I suspect they never thought seriously about divorce. They were committed to their marriage and determined to make it work.

Do you have any firm commitments? Because we have limited time and energies, we can't commit to too many things or relationships. But our lives will be empty if we don't take the risk of committing to something.

Difference makers are dedicated people, not afraid to

commit to a worthy cause. Christian difference makers are committed to a person, Jesus Christ. Our goal is to know him, to obey him, to become like him. Other commitments are important, but all are secondary to our commitment to Christ.

Humility. Prior to the 1988 election of George Bush as president of the United States, a host of aspiring politicians got into the race for the White House. At one point, fifteen candidates were actively pursuing a powerful position that most of us wouldn't want.

One by one, the candidates dropped out of the running. Whenever they did, each made a public statement. I can remember only one. Perhaps with a touch of bitterness, the withdrawing candidate concluded that a person has to be crazy, a masochist, and an egomaniac to run for president in the American system. Of course the job has perks and power along with the pressures, but for several months before the election, candidates must tear around the country and appear on television with a similar message: "Look at me. I'm the best! There is no better person for this job."

One former president, Abraham Lincoln, is particularly admired for his humility, but we seem to have few genuinely humble leaders in government today. The situation is just as bad in the business world, educational institutions, and even in many churches.

True humility is an attitude that keeps life in its proper perspective. Humble people do not ignore the existence of God or live as if they can get along fine without him. Genuinely humble people do not assume that they are always right. Their opinions about the Bible and theology are open to correction, and they don't assume that anyone who disagrees with them is wrong.[12]

Those who are humble do not demean or deny their God-given abilities and accomplishments. Humble people realize, instead, that all we have and achieve comes because of the goodness of God. Like Job, humble people know that the Lord gives and can as easily take away.

In a democracy, candidates for any office must convince voters of their ability to lead. Some do this without boasting or making exaggerated claims of their self-importance. Humble and effective difference makers, like good leaders, accept compliments graciously but don't dwell on them or take them too seriously. Such people try to learn from reasonable criticism and avoid blaming or harping on the mistakes of others.

Paul the apostle was a humble man. He freely acknowledged his failures and weaknesses, but he didn't keep dwelling on his inadequacies. Instead he acknowledged that his strength and calling came from God, and he served as effectively as he could. At the end of life he could look back and say, "I have fought the good fight, I have finished the course." With God's help, he had done his best and made a difference.

Humility is more than a characteristic that we strive to possess; humility is something we do. We humble ourselves before God and before other people.[13] We strive to keep a balanced perspective on our own strengths and accomplishments. We remind ourselves, and we remind each other, that God esteems those who are not proud[14] and is most inclined to use people who sincerely seek to be humble.

Willingness to learn. Kenneth Kantzer is one of my heroes. He might find that surprising.

When I was a young professor with some theological training but without a theological degree, Dr. Kantzer was willing to hire me for a position at a theological school. My job was to teach pastoral counseling to seminary students on their way to the ministry. This was a challenge for me, in part because I was in a graduate school that was new, growing, exciting, and on the cutting edge of theological education. The faculty was small, innovative, sometimes abrasive in their enthusiasm, but committed to making their institution the best in the nation. Kenneth Kantzer was the dean.

Over the years he inspired me with his consistent commitment to scholarship, his emphasis on personal piety, and his persistence in molding a school step by step. At times he made mistakes, and sometimes he made us angry. But he was always open to new ideas and willing to meet with me to talk about my career, my work at the school, and my family.

After he retired and a new dean took over, Ken Kantzer became senior editor of *Christianity Today* magazine. After five productive years, he retired from that position and took over as president of a struggling college that seemed destined for collapse. When he finished seeing that crisis through (the school survived), he returned to the seminary to head the development of a PhD program in theology.

Around that time I was teaching a course on the psychology of aging. My students had visited a couple of old people's homes and we had focused on the problems of the elderly. But the students wanted exposure to some senior citizen who was still active, who wasn't confined to a nursing home or sitting all day in a rocker. I cringed when somebody suggested that we should invite Dr. Kantzer to talk with the class about being old. I wondered how this humble but distinguished man would respond if we asked him to be an exhibit for our study of the elderly. I tried to convince the students that he probably was too busy, that they should invite some retired person with nothing better to do.

But the students insisted on inviting the Kantzers. I'm glad they did. Our ninety-minute meeting with Kenneth and Ruth Kantzer stands out as one of the highest points in my teaching career. Once again I saw a man who had clear convictions but who respected and didn't put down people with whom he disagreed. He showed my students that he still reads widely, is open to new ideas, is always learning, and is creatively planning for the future, even though he and his wife are well into their seventies. Mrs. Kantzer gently showed the students what my wife and I have seen often over the years: a woman whose compassion, sharp thinking, and sensitivity have helped hundreds of students and their spouses, even as she has consistently supported, encouraged, and challenged her better-known husband. Perhaps the open, always learning mentality that we saw in that class discussion helps to explain why Kenneth Kantzer and his wife have been long-term difference makers.

Rigid, narrow minded, non-thinking people rarely make much of a difference. When we stay within our own denominations, talk only to people in our own professions, avoid non-Christians, or close our minds to new ways of thinking, we soon find ourselves cut off from fresh ideas and stimulating new friendships. We dry up mentally when our worlds are no larger than a small circle of friends or our interests go no further than the images on a television screen. In time, creativity fades away and a mental rigor mortis sets in, long before we are ready to die. In contrast, when we are open to new ideas, we discover fresh opportunities and see new possibilities for making a difference.

When Paul was in Athens, waiting for his two friends to arrive, he went to the synagogue, spent time in the marketplace, talked with the people, looked carefully at their objects of worship, and even learned a little about their poetry. Paul kept learning, and his new knowledge was useful when an invitation came to address the wise men of Athens. Some of these local leaders sneered when he told them about the resurrection, but others believed. Would they have given him a hearing if Paul had kept a closed mind and not bothered to keep learning?[15] Even when he was in prison at the end of his life, Paul wrote asking Timothy to bring parchments and books. The old apostle was still learning and willing to grow.[16]

Daniel took time to learn the literature and language of the Babylonians. Joseph learned about Egyptian politics, agriculture, government administration, and interpersonal relations. The book of Proverbs is filled with wisdom designed, in part, to add to our storehouse of knowledge. Even Jesus, God's Son, spent years growing in wisdom and knowledge.

In Bible times, life was simpler. It may have been easier to keep informed. In contrast, we live in complex societies and are swamped with waves of the facts and opinions that make this the information age. In some places the Sunday paper is so huge that we couldn't read it through, even if we took all week. It is difficult for any of us to keep abreast of change. Few of us even try.

But people who make a difference keep reading and determine not to slip into mental flabbiness. When ninety difference makers were asked to list the personal qualities needed to run their organizations, nobody mentioned charisma, dressing for success, or time management. They talked instead about persistence, commitment, and a willingness to take risks. Most of all, they talked about learning, including the need to read. Learning for these people was like a high-octane fuel that kept them sharp, open to new ideas, creative, and able to make a significant difference in their world.[17]

In one of his books, Gordon MacDonald wrote about the times he has visited with pastors who feel ineffective and struggle with feelings of failure. Almost always, these people have stopped reading. When they stop reading, they stop growing. Often they also stop thinking and they grow dependent on the thoughts and opinions of others. Instead of dealing with ideas and issues, these weary Christian

leaders limit their thinking and narrow their preaching to
irrelevant viewpoints, simplistic ideas, and a focus on rules
and rigid regulations. Their lives, their minds, and their
churches all become empty.

You don't have to be an intellectual to be a difference
maker; neither do you have to be an avid reader. But people
who make a difference are open to new ideas, willing to
change, and not afraid to learn. Many realize that by
pursuing truth, developing a humble attitude, living out
their commitments, and acting with integrity, they will not
be easily entangled by the sin that can keep them from
being effective difference makers.

Chapter Highlights

‡ Sin can get in the way of difference making. To be
  effective we need to look carefully at our lives, admit
  and confess our sins, and shed behavior and attitudes
  that can hinder our difference-making activities.
‡ As we pursue integrity, commitment, humility, and a
  willingness to learn, sin is less likely to trip us up.

6

Pursue Clear Goals

Hoshino Tomihiro was in primary school when he saw gymnastics for the first time. His young eyes had never feasted on anything like it, and he remembered every detail: the body clad in a pure white athletic suit jumping high and spinning in the air, the handstands, the graceful rotations on the horizontal bar. Hoshino made up his mind on the spot. He would become a gymnast.

The next day he tried it himself, flopping in a muddy paddy field recently cleared of its rice crop. There were no parallel bars or exercise mats in the tiny mountain village where he lived and nobody encouraged the young Japanese as he practiced by himself in the fields.

All of this changed when he got to high school. Immediately he joined the gymnastics club and for seven years, until his graduation from Gumma University, he practiced gymnastics. When a teaching job became available at Kuragano Junior High School in Takasaki City, he accepted, not because he wanted to teach but because he wanted a place to pursue his love of gymnastics. He was good. Others would watch in awe, as he had watched so many years ago, while his white-clad body spun in the air and landed gracefully on the mat below.

All of this ended abruptly when Hoshino Tomihiro broke his neck.

His limp body was lifted gently to the stretcher and rushed to the hospital. The days that followed were a blur of confusion and pain. His temperature shot up to 104 and stayed there. He had trouble breathing, couldn't urinate, and was unable to move from the neck down. More than once the doctors told his family to call the relatives and prepare for his imminent death.

But Hoshino Tomihiro survived. For nine years he remained in that hospital, sustained in part by a loving mother, a compassionate medical staff, and a few faithful friends. One brought a Bible, and after weeks of hesitation, the young man began to read. Eventually he became a Christian.

Another friend put a pen in Hoshino's mouth one day and urged him to make a mark on a souvenir hat that had been signed by everyone on the ward and was being sent to a former patient. With Herculean effort, the young man clenched the pen in his teeth and made the mark. Nobody would have guessed that this simple act would start the long, slow process of learning to paint flowers with a brush held between his teeth. In time an exhibition was held in Tokyo and books illustrated by the young artist's paintings appeared in the bookstores.

I bought one of these in Japan and learned, as I read, about a man whose life has involved many years of patiently and persistently moving toward goals. He lives away from the hospital now in a specially designed wheel chair that he drives himself, holding the controls in his mouth. Encouraged by his wife, a Christian lady who once was his nurse, Mr. Tomihiro has displayed his paintings in thirty cities throughout Japan. His books have brought inspiration to thousands.[1]

Hoshino Tomihiro is a difference maker because he dared to set some goals and persisted until he reached them. He follows the exhortation found in Hebrews 12:1: "Let us run with perseverance."

Principle Number Three:
Set Some Goals and Stick With Them

A newsletter recently carried a sketch of men and women walking quickly in a big circle. Each was following the person in front. One of the marchers commented to another, "I sure hope the person at the head of this line knows where we are going."

Do you ever feel like that, as though life is a steady march in a big circle going nowhere? Effective Christians don't go in circles. They are running a race with clear goals and with their daily lives in contact with Jesus.

Not long ago I was sitting in an airplane, engrossed in a book, when I read this sentence: "Try to see the world simultaneously as it is and as it can be." When I read that sentence, I turned to the inside back cover of the book and drew a line to make two columns. At the top I wrote "the way it is" and "the way it can be." Then I started to make my lists.

Sometimes little exercises like this can help us dream dreams and plan for the future. When we have committed our lives to the leading of God and we genuinely want his guidance, we can plan creatively and expect that he will guide our steps.[2]

Lee Strobel was the legal editor of the *Chicago Tribune* and a strong atheist when his wife, Leslie, told him about Christ. For almost two years the resistant young editor investigated the claims of the Gospel, applying his journalistic skills and his legal training with deliberate and painstaking study. When he was convinced that he should become a Christian, Lee Strobel put his faith in Christ and began to thrive spiritually. Because of his careful investigation, he knew what he believed and why.

In the months that followed, this new believer wondered if he would ever be able to present the good news of Jesus Christ to others, maybe even to large groups. In time he resigned from the newspaper staff, accepted a salary cut, and took a new job on the staff of a local church. There he was asked to speak, and now his messages have been helpful to thousands—including me. Lee Strobel is making a difference.

Recently he suggested a helpful three-part formula for finding and developing one's potential.[3] First, we need to set some goals. Ask yourself what really excites you. If the sky was the limit, what would you really like to accomplish? Are these goals clearly consistent with biblical teaching? Ask God to show you which goals to pursue. When you are ready, talk to another mature Christian about your aspirations and get some feedback. If your goals enable you to serve people and honor Christ, you probably are on the right track. If the goals are more likely to build your influence and ego, reconsider them. It might be wise to forget them.

Second, think about a game plan. Pick one or two goals, ask God to guide your thinking, and decide on some steps to help you reach these goals. Remember, you make a difference by taking one small step at a time. You might also tell a few supportive, praying friends what you are doing. You don't have to tell everybody.

Third, think about your gifts, abilities, and personality. God is most likely to use us in ways that spark our interests and that accentuate the abilities he has given us.

By starting small, you can test out your ideas, skills, and abilities. God puts us in charge of greater things when we have proven to be faithful in small things.[4]

In all of this, try to be realistic. God doesn't expect all of us to accomplish impressive feats. Sometimes we do great things for God even though they are not widely noticed or acclaimed by others. At times little things make the greatest difference.

Sticking with your goals. If you have even a passing acquaintance with football, you probably have heard of the Chicago Bears. But have you heard about the Moscow Bears?

Until recently American football was largely unknown in the Soviet Union, but some enterprising individual got the idea of preparing a Russian team and sending it to play exhibition games in the United States. A former coach of the Denver Broncos was hired to coach the new team, but they had a few difficulties.

Quarterback Yuri Boldin had never held a football until seven months before the start of the tour. His teammates were equally inexperienced. Because none of the Russians understood English, interpreters had to be present both during training and alongside officials on the football field once the games started.

When the team arrived in Tacoma, Washington, for the first-ever game of the Soviet Union American Football League, the stadium was filled to capacity. The local band played the Star Spangled Banner along with the Turkish national anthem. The band members thought they were playing the Soviet national anthem, but somebody had accidentally mixed up the music.

From the start, the minor league Tacoma Express outplayed the visitors, so the enthusiastic local crowd began chanting an enthusiastic "Go Bears!" When the locals scored first, the visitors kept playing as hard as they could. They continued without letup through all four quarters. Next morning, newspapers applauded the Soviets for their persistence and determination. Some reporters were even diplomatic enough to make no mention of the final score.

It was a little lopsided. The visitors lost 61-0.

Those young players impressively demonstrated their determination, however.[5] Some of them may have enough persistence to keep practicing until they develop their skills and learn how to play well.

The same is true as we run the race of life. Even when there are setbacks, we must run with perseverance. The Greek word for perseverance means both a passive endurance, despite what happens, and an active determination to persist and to keep going. Difference makers persevere.

Model Difference Makers

Several years ago, British journalist Malcolm Muggeridge led a BBC television team to India where they were to film a documentary on Mother Teresa. Muggeridge had once lived in Calcutta, so he was familiar with the heat, the filth, and the misery. But he was not prepared for the dedication of the frail nun from Yugoslavia and her associates. They persisted in the never-ending task of working with the poor and terminally ill in the Calcutta slums. They demonstrated "a spirit so indomitable, a faith so intractable, a love so abounding," that Malcolm Muggeridge was overwhelmed.

As the film crew followed Mother Teresa while she worked, Muggeridge found himself going through a change. At first there was horror mixed with pity in what he saw. Then came compassion, followed by something that the hardened journalist had never experienced before: "An awareness that these dying and derelict men and women, these lepers with stumps instead of hands, these unwanted children, were not pitiable, repulsive or forlorn, but rather dear and delightful; as it might be, friends of long standing, brothers and sisters."[6]

Mother Teresa began her work with a dream and with only a few rupees in her pocket. She waited two years for permission to be released from her vows so she could go back into the world to pursue her goal of ministering to the poor. Winning a Nobel Prize never entered her mind, and she probably was realistic enough to know that her efforts wouldn't make a dent in the massive misery of Calcutta. But she persevered.

Perseverance toward worthy goals pleases God. He expects perseverance, knows about it, and rewards it.[7] Perseverance builds character, especially when we persevere in the midst of difficult conditions.[8] Difference makers set goals and persevere in reaching them.

The Old Testament book of Esther is an exciting drama, woven around a conflict between two men. Mordecai was a Jewish man of no particular note, who once overheard two individuals planning the king's assassination. Mordecai got word to the king, the plotters were arrested and hanged, and the faithful informer went back to sitting in the market.

Haman, the other man in the story, was the king's drinking buddy. Cocky and boastful, Haman expected people to bow when he rode through the streets. When Mordecai refused to do so, Haman began to plot how he could exterminate both Mordecai and the entire Jewish nation. Haman built a huge gallows for Mordecai and convinced the king to issue an extermination order.

Neither Haman nor King Xerxes knew that the queen was Jewish and related to Mordecai. While the Jews wept at the news of the king's order, Mordecai approached Queen Esther and told her that she alone could plead for the lives of her people.

This was a dangerous suggestion. The Persian court had a rule that no person could speak to the king unless bidden. To appear without being called could mean immediate death.

What happened next is well known. Esther approached the king. The extermination order was rescinded, Haman was hanged on his own gallows, and Mordecai was elevated to a position of prominence.

In reading this story recently, I noticed some traits in

Esther and Mordecai that could explain why they were used by God to be difference makers. First, they had an expectancy. "If you remain silent at this time," Mordecai said, "relief and deliverance for the Jews will arise from another place."⁹ Even if some might perish in the meantime, it never occurred to Mordecai that God wouldn't do something to save his people and to stop the king's order.

Second, these people had a *sense of destiny*, a belief that God's hand was on their lives and giving them opportunities to be difference makers. Mordecai's question to the queen is the most famous quotation from the entire book: "Who knows but that you have come to royal position for such a time as this?"

Third, throughout the drama, there is a *submission to God*. These people prayed and fasted for three days before taking action. Clearly they wanted divine blessing and guidance as they launched their plan.

Finally, there was a *willingness to take a risk*. Queen Esther knew that her plan to approach the king was dangerous, but she announced her decision to Mordecai: "I will go to the king, even though it is against the law. And if I perish, I perish."

This drama of Esther and Mordecai seems strangely out of place in the contemporary world where you and I live. What could we learn by looking so far back into history when we live in a high-tech, rapidly changing information age?

Of course the world changes constantly, but we need to remember that God does not. Sometimes he seems silent and far away, but if he is truly God—all powerful, all knowing, and omnipresent—then he has not withdrawn from the universe to leave us on our own. He who created the world still sustains it and watches over it.¹⁰ Nothing in creation is hidden from God's sight.¹¹ He is aware of us as individuals. He knows our needs, the details of our lives, even our thoughts and hidden motives.[12]

Throughout the Bible, we see examples of God working through individuals. Most often they seemed unlikely candidates to be God's chosen instruments and sometimes they were surprised. Few had heard of Mordecai or Esther when their adventure began. Yet even as God worked through Mordecai and Esther, he can work through us today.[13] And who knows, *you* may be where you are "for such a time as this."

Please stop to think about that!

No individual is left to drift uselessly through life. Some of us may have such terrible self-concepts and such small views of God that we see no way in which he could use us. Maybe we believe that he intervened in history and in people's lives many years ago but doubt that he does that any longer. Often we don't expect God to lead, so we miss his direction.

We can still learn from Mordecai and Esther. They looked at their world and at their lives. They bounced ideas off each other, considered possibilities, made a decision about what to do, cautiously moved in that direction, and were willing to take risks. All of this was surrounded by prayer and undergirded by an unwavering spiritual commitment. It isn't surprising that their actions made a difference.

Chapter Highlights

‡ Effective Christians don't go around in circles. They are running a race with clear goals and with their daily lives in contact with Jesus.

‡ To make a difference, set some goals and stick with them, even when that isn't easy.

‡ The Old Testament book of Esther shows us how we can be used by God to change people's lives.

Focus Your Life on Christ

When an aging member of the royal family of South Africa's Xhosa tribe came to North America, he took the place by storm. He addressed the Parliament of Canada and the Congress of the United States, rode in a New York City ticker-tape parade, and appeared on the front pages of all our newspapers.

Why was Nelson Mandela lauded as a hero, even though his message was not always popular and his methods were criticized in the press and in the halls of government? One congressman tried to answer. Mandela, he said, came as a man with principles. He knew what he stood for and he refused to be swayed from his life purpose. For twenty-seven years he had stayed in jail, unwilling to compromise his standards even to gain release. Like Gandhi, Martin Luther King, Jr., Lech Walesa, and Vaclac Havel, Mandela emerged from his prison cell and regally mounted the podiums of the world to proclaim his message without fear, hesitation, or compromise. Clearly, he has made a difference.

All of us admire people like that, even when we might disagree with their politics or convictions. When pollsters conduct surveys to find the world's most admired people, the names of Billy Graham, Pope John Paul II, and Mother Teresa appear consistently. Each of these people has firm convictions. None is willing to compromise. They stand up and are counted. They are not ashamed to take a position, however unpopular, even when they are surrounded by critics and cynics.

Jesus was like that; so were Paul and the other apostles. We should follow their example.

In reality, however, many Christians keep their convictions hidden. We claim to be believers, and we are, but we don't want to appear intolerant or hyper-religious. We don't want anyone to think that we're narrow-minded fundamentalists, Bible-thumpers, theological liberals or ultra-conservatives, or in any way associated with the followers of some television evangelist. Sometimes we become very busy distancing ourselves from the Christians whom we don't admire. In the process, nobody knows whom we admire and where we stand. We may not even know ourselves.

No runner completes a marathon by looking around and making comparisons with others. The successful runner has a goal, to reach the finish line. He or she is not dissuaded by distractions. If other runners stumble or do something stupid, especially when they are passing the crowds or television cameras, the marathoner keeps going. If the crowds jeer or try to be distracting, the runner does not break stride. Everyone can see that the long-distance runner is on a steady course, regardless of what the spectators may think or what the other runners may do.

Christian difference makers are like that. In running the race of life, we always remember that we are followers of Jesus. We "fix our eyes on Jesus, the author and perfecter of our faith" (Hebrews 12:2).

Principle Number Four: Fix Your Eyes on Jesus

This principle sounds admirable, but is it attainable? When we live our lives day by day, striving to survive but hoping to make a difference along the way, isn't it a lot easier to fix our eyes on our careers, our checkbooks, or our anxieties? How can we "fix our eyes on Jesus"? What does that mean?

Perhaps the answer can be found in two simple statements: We need to know him. We need to obey him.

We need to know him. For over twenty-five years, Jerry Bridges worked in a full-time Christian ministry both overseas and in North America. During that time he met many talented and capable Christians who were interested in serving God and accomplishing things for him. It was much rarer to find godly Christians who were interested in really knowing him.[1]

Throughout my lifetime, I have heard many sermons about what God can do for me and about what I can do for God. Christian books are filled with quick, easy, often superficial solutions to the problems of life, but there is little emphasis on the gradual, sometimes difficult task of knowing God better and becoming more like Christ.

It appears, however, that God himself is most interested in having us know him and his son Jesus Christ.[2] Enoch was a preacher of righteousness in a grossly unrighteous age, but the brief accounts of his life emphasize that he walked with God and pleased God.[3] The prophet Jeremiah wrote, "This is what the LORD says: 'Let not the wise man boast of his wisdom or the strong man boast of his strength or the rich man boast of his riches, but let him who boasts boast about this: *that he understands and knows me,* that I am the LORD, who exercises kindness, justice and righteousness on earth, for in these I delight,' declares the LORD."[4]

Knowing God may sound like a lofty idea, fine for Enoch and Jeremiah, but far removed from most of us and not much related to being a difference maker. Of course nobody can know God completely. Our minds are too tiny for that. But when we make the effort to know him better, we become more aware of what he is like and more inclined to be the difference makers that he wants us to be.

Knowing God involves:

‡ Reading the Bible and asking the Holy Spirit to help us understand it and apply it to our lives;

‡ Looking for his characteristics as they are revealed in Scripture;

‡ Expressing praise and appreciation for what God is like (even before we thank him for what he has done for us);

‡ Having a willingness to do what he commands.

If you are a high-energy person like I am, or if you are a very busy person like almost everybody, it is difficult to fit knowing God into your schedule. How, then, can we do this?

I hesitate to describe what I do, because that may not be best for you. I'm still learning how to know God, and there is no right technique or perfect formula. Even so, the example of somebody else can be helpful, especially if you modify it to fit your unique situation or personality characteristics.[5]

I schedule an appointment with God each day. Because I am a morning person, I usually shower and go immediately to a desk where I spend time quietly alone before the phone starts ringing or I get distracted by other things.

I try not to be rigid. Almost always, I start by asking God to show me what he is like, to teach me what I need to know, to keep my mind from wandering. (To help with that I try to keep away from a cluttered desk that might beckon me to other things.) Usually I read a chapter each from the Old Testament and the New Testament and supplement this with a psalm or some of the proverbs.

For several years I have kept a journal where I record my reactions to the events of my life and in the world, describe some of my travels, express my frustrations, map out my plans, and record what I have been learning from the Bible, from my readings, or from some recent sermon. I don't try to write in my journal every day, and often I will write at some time other than during my time alone with God in the morning.

Almost every day I write a prayer. I take about a page of my notebook and begin by thinking about some characteristics of God. I record these, thank God for them, and sometimes look into the Bible (especially the Psalms) to find others. Only then do I write confessions about my sins, thank God for what he has done, and jot down some prayer requests or the names of people for whom I want to pray. Of course, everything is not put on paper. Often I put down the pen and pray about some issue that has come to mind. But for me, the act of writing focuses my attention and keeps my active mind from wandering.

In all of this, I try not to be so busy that I don't have time to listen to what God wants me to hear. Usually such thoughts are triggered as I read the Bible or write my prayer.

This time of withdrawal gets me started on the day and sets the tone for the activities that follow. If I miss my morning appointment, I try not to get upset. But I discipline myself so that I don't miss too many days, and I almost never allow myself to push the snooze button on the clock and stay in bed through this quiet time. Many years ago I learned that the battle of the morning is won the night before. If I get to bed early enough, I am more inclined to get up in time to meet with God before I go to work.

Most of us agree that prayer is important, but our prayerless lives betray what we really believe: Doing things is more important than knowing God and finding time to spend with him.

A few miles from our home is a large and exciting church that attracts international attention. Every year the church hosts a series of conferences for pastors and other Christian leaders who want to make a difference and see their ministries grow. Participants sometimes travel great distances for the conference. They come expectantly, with enthusiasm, and with a readiness to receive new ideas. Some are surprised and a little disappointed by the core message: Real growth does not come from programs or gimmicks. Success flows from spiritual depth in church leaders and in the congregations they lead. When pastor and people are devoted above all else to worshiping God and knowing him better, the church begins to make a real difference and the people are able to serve God strategically.[6]

If you want to be a Christian difference maker, getting to know God is the most important thing you can do.

We need to obey him. On the week before the Crucifixion, Jesus had some long talks with his disciples.[7] He knew what was coming and wanted to give final directions to this little band who would take over after he left.

During this teaching, Jesus made a remarkable statement: "Apart from me you can do nothing." The words were barely out of his mouth when he told his hearers that they should be doing something—bearing much fruit—and in this way show themselves to be his disciples.[8]

God wants us to be productive for him, but we can't do that by ourselves. To be authentic Christian difference makers, we must be loving and obedient. Jesus repeated this message often. It makes no sense to call him Lord and fail to do what he says. It is futile to hear his words and not put them into practice. We cannot claim to be his followers if we rarely show love. But if we love him we will keep his commandments.[9]

Obedience to what the Scriptures teach is not optional for the person who wants to become a genuine difference maker who pleases God.

Each of us performs before three audiences in life: we continually evaluate ourselves, we are evaluated by others, and our lives are always seen by God. All three audiences are important for difference makers, but our most important audience is God. Ignore that audience, and you limit your potential to make a genuine and lasting difference.

Chapter Highlights

‡ The most effective difference makers keep their eyes on Jesus, taking the time and effort to know him better. They are determined to obey his commands.

‡ Each of us performs before three audiences: ourselves, others, and God. If you want to make a long-lasting difference, don't forget your most important audience: God.

8

Expect Resistance

Every half hour or so, especially during the summer, a tour bus makes its way through a quiet neighborhood in Nashville and turns onto Curtiswood Drive. The curious passengers strain to see two attractions that sit side by side: the opulent governor's mansion and the house next door where a gracious and refined lady named Sarah Cannon has lived for more than twenty years.

Sarah grew up in a small Tennessee community and joined a touring drama company more than fifty years ago. When the group reached a secluded mountain town in north Alabama, far from any motels, Sarah was put up in a tiny cabin with a delightful little lady who told endless hillbilly tales to her fascinated guest.

Sarah came away imitating her hostess, and the people in the touring group roared with good-natured laughter. It wasn't long before Sarah took her act on stage. She played to rave reviews before the local Lion's Club and a banker's convention, but the pay wasn't very good, she didn't have a steady job, and she hadn't realized that show business can be a tough business. At twenty-seven she thought her career was over, but then came her big break. She was invited to audition for a famous country music show and was given the opportunity to perform late one Saturday night. The lady was an immediate show business success.

Shortly after her fiftieth birthday, Sarah began to experience a painful arthritis. Several years later she developed cancer and faced a double mastectomy. Despite these setbacks she kept performing, encouraged by her strong Christian faith and by the man who has been her husband for more than forty years.

When asked how she would like to be remembered, Mrs. Cannon quoted from memory: "I shall pass through this world but once. Therefore, if there's any good that I can do, I must do it now, not defer nor neglect it, for I shall not pass this way again."

Then she added, "If you've had a life-threatening disease, which arthritis isn't but cancer is, you want to be sure that you get the most out of life and do the most you can for others. I feel that I was left here for a reason."

Now in her late seventies, Sarah Cannon is still a difference maker. For half a century she has brought laughter into the lives of millions, including many of those people on the tour buses. They know Sarah Cannon by her stage name:

The Grand Ole Opry's Minnie Pearl.[1]

Difference makers like Minnie Pearl often face resistance. The writer of Hebrews reminds us of the hardships that Jesus faced: "Consider him who endured such opposition from sinful men, so that you will not grow weary and lose heart. . . . Endure hardship as discipline; God is treating you as sons."[2]

Principle Number Five:
Expect Resistance

During a visit overseas, I once met a man who described his countrymen as having a lawn-mower mentality.

"We don't much like to see people get ahead," my friend explained. "If anybody does something to stand out from the crowd, we do to that person what the lawn mower does to a blade of grass that grows taller than the others. We cut the one that rises higher down to the same size as all the rest."

Then he added a thoughtful comment. "Our best people

get frustrated, so they go abroad to achieve success. Then we pile on criticism because they have forsaken their homeland."

Citizens in that country with the lawn-mower thinking have faced opposition and criticism from their fellow countrymen. History books are filled with the names of difference makers who suffered and encountered resistance. But nobody faced obstruction, hardship, struggle, scorn, suffering, and bloodshed like Jesus Christ, the greatest difference maker of all. If we are serious about making a difference, we can expect to encounter resistance.

As followers of Christ, we not only run a race as we go through life; we run through an obstacle course. And God is the source of some of the obstacles. Just as a loving father disciplines his children, so a loving heavenly father corrects his sons and daughters. That isn't pleasant; no discipline is. But the suffering and pain is for our benefit. It enables us to become more holy and it trains us to be better, more effective race runners and difference makers.[3]

Like believers today, Christians in the early church sometimes lost their freshness and enthusiasm. Instead of running strongly, they were feeble and tottered with weak knees. Some had been persecuted. Many may have felt defeated and disabled. The words from Hebrews that encouraged them can bring us hope during times of difficulty.

An ancient tale with a modern message. Many years before the letter to Hebrews was written, King Artaxerxes of Babylon had a cup bearer, a foreigner named Nehemiah whose job was to bring wine to the king. In those days, royal employees were expected to put on a happy face when they came into the court, but Nehemiah was not able to hide his sadness, and the king noticed.

"Why does your face look so sad?" Nehemiah was asked. He replied by telling the king about the people in

Jerusalem. They were living in trouble, disgrace, and danger. Their lives were filled with suffering and obstacles.

King Artaxerxes temporarily released Nehemiah from his duties and gave him permission to go back to Jerusalem to rebuild the city wall. In those days, travelers journeyed by horseback. The trip probably took from three to four months. Nehemiah was both tired and sad when he reached Jerusalem and saw his hometown lying in ruins.

But Nehemiah was a difference maker. He had prayed about this mission, and he was ready for the challenge. The king had given military protection for the journey, help in acquiring the needed supplies, and a letter to the local governor authorizing the work to begin.

It began in earnest. So, too, did the resistance.

First came ridicule and a suggestion that Nehemiah was guilty of rebelling against the king. Nehemiah responded by ignoring the jokes and expressing his confidence in God.

And the rebuilding of the wall continued.

Next the critics plotted to fight against the wall builders and tried to stir up trouble. Nehemiah responded with prayer. Then his people posted a guard.

And the rebuilding of the wall continued.

Is it surprising that the next obstacle came from sheer exhaustion? The strength of the laborers began to give out and there was fear that the opposition would overtake the weary workers while their resistance was down. So Nehemiah gave an inspirational speech, reminding the people about their awesome God. Then they divided the workers into two groups. While half were doing hard physical labor, the other half stood guard equipped with swords, shields, and other weapons.

And the rebuilding of the wall continued.

The next obstacle came from inside. Some of the wall builders were taking financial advantage of their fellow laborers. As a result many of the workers had no money for food or accommodations. There was complaining, anger, discouragement, and a sense of injustice among people who should have been working together.

Nehemiah was angry when he heard about this, but instead of over-reacting, he took time to ponder what should be done. A short time later he called everybody to a meeting and demanded that there be financial justice within the ranks. His remarks were especially powerful because Nehemiah was able to show that he himself had been fair and remarkably generous with his employees. As a result, justice was restored. The unethical business practices stopped.

And the rebuilding of the wall continued.

So the critics tried to entrap Nehemiah by luring him away from the task and tripping up his clear thinking. But Nehemiah resisted the bait. He kept aware of his mission and refused to be dissuaded from his goals. "I am carrying on a great project," he said. There was no time for getting distracted. Nehemiah kept things in perspective, even as he continued to ask for God's wisdom and guidance.

And the rebuilding of the wall continued.

Finally, there were shrewd attempts to lure Nehemiah into compromising situations where he would be guilty of breaking God's laws. This has always been one of the Devil's most powerful tactics: taking what is wrong and making it look like something that is right, luring believers into intimidating situations. Nehemiah responded with courage and a renewed determination to be obedient.[4]

And the building of the wall was completed.

Difference makers should not be surprised when opposition comes. We can expect it. When it comes, especially when the opposition is unexpected and undeserved, we can respond in one of four ways. We can respond like most people do, with retaliation and revenge. We can respond like the Thessalonians who were alarmed because they thought their suffering meant that they were out of God's will—even though they weren't.[5] We can respond like the Hebrew Christians who considered abandoning their faith when the heat was on.[6] Or we can respond like Jesus who entrusted his unfair treatment to God and returned love for hatred.[7]

Like Nehemiah, we can handle and overcome the resistance. Nehemiah was surrounded by others who believed as he did. Undoubtedly they encouraged one another. He and his colleagues worked hard to reach their goal without wavering. They kept alert to the opposition and were not distracted by the obstacles in their path. Most important, they remembered that they had a great and powerful God who was in control. And they were led by a godly man of prayer.

Despite obstacles, you can be a difference maker when you walk in close communion with Christ, keeping your eyes on him so that you don't grow weary, lose heart, and give up.

Chapter Highlights

‡ People who make a difference are likely to encounter resistance. They can expect difficulties and sometimes criticism.

9

Build Long-term
Relationships

I've never met Kenneth T. Wessner. He and I are members of
the same church and I have seen him from a distance, but
our congregation is large and it isn't easy for one person to
meet everybody else. On occasion his picture appears in the
business section of the newspaper, but most of his fellow
worshipers probably are unaware of this man's influence as a
difference maker in the corporate world.

Until his retirement, Ken Wessner was chairman of the
ServiceMaster Company, a two-and-a-half billion dollar
corporation that began in 1947 as a small business cleaning
rugs and furniture in homes and offices around suburban
Chicago. Founded by a Baptist, a Roman Catholic, and a
Presbyterian, the name ServiceMaster was chosen to de-
scribe the company's ultimate purpose: service to the
Master.

As the company grew, so did its clientele and range of
services. Today, ServiceMaster is worldwide. In the United
States alone, it serves over 1,400 health care facilities by
managing their plant operations—maintenance, clinical
equipment, housekeeping, laundry, and food service. Over
600 colleges, universities, and public school systems have
ServiceMaster managing their custodial, grounds care, and
plant operations, including maintenance and food services.
These same services are managed in several hundred large,
industrial plants. Together, roughly 10,000 managers and
over 200,000 workers perform the various ServiceMaster
services.

But that isn't all. In addition to management services, the company provides consumer services that include: over 5000 licensed ServiceMaster professional cleaners of homes and offices, Merry Maids, Tru-Green lawn care, American Home Shield, and Terminex, the world's largest pest-control termite business.

As a company, ServiceMaster has made a difference, in part because of its emphasis on people. According to Ken Wessner, the company has four objectives: "To honor God in all we do. To help people develop. To pursue excellence. To grow profitably." The corporate vision is stated with equal precision: "To be an ever-expanding and vital market vehicle for use by God to work in the lives of people as they serve and contribute to others."

These are more than empty words hanging in a frame on some boardroom wall. "Our corporate objectives are very much a part of us," Wessner told a reporter. "It is important for us to keep our four objectives in balance, and the ultimate dignity of people is expressed in our vision statement. These two written statements have helped us to think what kind of a company we want to be and what kind of people we want to be."

William Pollard, the present company chairman, echoes that sentiment. "We really do what the name suggests, service to the Master," he said. "It's part of us and the jobs we do. Our company cannot grow if the people in our company are not able to grow in every way. We're a company of people."[1]

Ken Wessner and his colleagues are difference makers. They make a difference because they are dedicated to serving the Master with work of the highest quality and they are committed to encouraging and building people.

Principle Number Six:
Build Relationships

None of us will be difference makers for God if we forget people and are insensitive to their needs. When she was a teenager, one of our daughters came home from a trip to the supermarket with a bag full of groceries and a body trembling with anger over the insensitivity of some fellow grocery shoppers. A wizened little old man had been holding up the line because he couldn't find enough food stamps to cover his purchases.

"He was old and confused," my daughter reported, "but the impatient and self-centered people at the check-out counter couldn't even wait a few minutes before making cynical and critical comments about the old guy who was causing them a minor inconvenience."

We both felt sorry for the old man. Even more, we felt sorry for the people in that line who couldn't be bothered to show patience and kindness to a human being in need of understanding and perhaps a little help.

Genuine kindness and sensitivity to people are not performances that we plan in advance, act out on occasion, and then forget. Sincere, authentic sensitivity comes from God, flows from within, and becomes part of our way of life.

The writer of Hebrews was concerned about sensitivity and relationships. After reading about the obstacles and suffering that Christians will face as they run the race of life, we read these words: "Make every effort to live in peace with all men."[2] Then we see three brief, perhaps surprising, clues about how this can be done: be holy, be free of bitterness, be pure.

Be holy. Is that possible? Is it realistic for people like us to strive for holiness? And suppose we could make progress in becoming holy. Wouldn't that make us dull and so irrelevant that we would be cut off from making a difference in the lives of more down-to-earth people?

According to Jerry Bridges, who wrote a whole book in response to Hebrews 12:14, "holiness is a process, something we never completely attain in this life." The command to pursue holiness suggests that this is a lifelong task involving diligence and consistent effort. "To live a holy life," Bridges wrote, "is to live in conformity to the moral precepts of the Bible and in contrast to the sinful ways of the world."[3]

Why should this interest difference makers? The Bible shows that holiness and usefulness are linked. When an individual fails to give serious attention to the process of becoming more holy, he or she cannot expect to be an effective Christian difference maker. Developing personal holiness must be a goal for any believer who wants to be "an instrument for noble purposes . . . useful to the Master and prepared to do any good work."[4]

How, then, do imperfect people like you and me become holy?

There are no simple answers, but to start, we must want it. God expects us to strive to be holy in all we do.[5] Sadly, this message often is ignored in our churches. More often we emphasize the benefits of our faith and proclaim a what's-in-it-for-me gospel while ignoring the importance of holy living. Rarely are we told that without holiness, we can't get close to God or see the Lord.[6]

To grow in holiness, we must ask God to help us both to want holiness and to make decisions that are consistent with his perfect will. We need to discipline ourselves to spend time with God in prayer and Bible reading. The more we know him, the more we can be like him. The more we are like him, the more we are holy. The more we are holy, the more we can be sensitive difference makers who touch the lives of others.

Be free of bitterness. Hebrews 12:15 makes the remarkable statement that bitterness can take root in a life and "grow up to cause trouble and defile many."

Several years ago, when I was preparing to revise a counseling book I had written,[7] the publisher sent a questionnaire to several hundred counselors, including pastors. We asked them to tell us the problems that are seen most often in their counselees. To our surprise, bitterness came near the top of the list.

People who are bitter feel intense animosity. They are unwilling to forgive and often their goal is to get even. Some bitter people make statements, spread gossip, or find ways to gain revenge. Others hold the bitterness inside and fantasize about getting even. When someone thinks like this, the one who is most likely to be hurt is the person who is bitter.

"Always give your best," Theodore Roosevelt once said. "Never get discouraged, never be petty. Always remember, others may hate you, but those that hate you don't win unless you hate them, and then you destroy yourself." Then you have undermined your ability to be a positive difference maker.

We've all been mistreated at times, and it isn't easy to forgive or forget. It is hard to let God bring justice; it is easier to plan vengeance ourselves. But God expects Christians to live in peace with others, to avoid revenge, to let him handle the accounts and bring justice, and—this is the difficult part—to treat our enemies with kindness.[8] The person who follows these principles will not fail to be a difference maker.

Be pure. Some time ago I had dinner with a young couple whose nationally-known pastor had been discovered in a motel room with a woman who was not his wife. Over dinner, my friends described the shock, anger, and despair that had settled over their congregation.

"He was our spiritual hero," the young husband told me. "We listened carefully to what he said. We believed his messages when he called for purity. And all this time he was shacking up in a motel room. His actions have demolished a lot of people. Some have become physical and spiritual wrecks because of what he did." At one time that pastor was a powerful and effective difference maker for Christ, but not any more.

Repeatedly, the Scriptures teach that we must avoid sexual immorality.[9] Perhaps this is mentioned so often because it is ignored so often!

Christ-honoring difference makers strive to be pure in their thinking, their talk, and their actions. These are people who feel the greatest freedom to make a difference. Because their lives are free of sexual immorality, there is no need to worry about somebody discovering a secret immoral relationship. These people don't have to carry a burden of guilt and unconfessed sin. They are free to be honest before God. There are no skeletons in their closets. They have nothing to hide from others. They are freed to be effective difference makers.

The apostle Paul wrote about this in one of his letters to the early churches. If we belong to Jesus Christ, if we make every effort to squelch our sinful passions, and if we keep in step with the Holy Spirit's guidance, then we are less inclined to be conceited, envious, and insensitive. Dedicated believers like this show evidence of the fruit of the Spirit: love, joy, peace, patience, kindness, goodness, faithfulness, gentleness, and self-control. There could be no better list of attributes for sensitive difference makers who are striving for purity.[10]

Obviously, there are some people who make profound changes in our world while remaining insensitive, self-centered, non-caring, and not much interested in purity.

These people leave a mark on future generations. But when the love of God enters their lives, they change.

Prior to Watergate, Charles Colson was described as President Nixon's "hatchet man." In those days before he became a Christian, Colson was a close associate of the president and a tough ex-Marine infantry captain who was not known for compassion and sensitivity. He made a difference, but he probably scarred many lives by his insensitivity and abrupt manner.

Then Charles Colson became a believer. He spent time in prison and saw, firsthand, some of the pain and despair of his fellow inmates. Eventually he founded an international organization, Prison Fellowship, that would meet spiritual, physical, and other needs of prisoners and their families.

After his life had been touched by God, the former hatchet-man became a genuinely compassionate, sensitive difference maker. Colson's energies are now devoted to helping others. His books have influenced millions. His life is dedicated to loving God and guiding others to do the same. He has turned from being an insensitive difference maker whose words and actions stung others, to being a sensitive difference maker who genuinely cares about others.[11]

People building. Caring for others and building relationships often involve encouraging growth in people around us. W. Steven Brown is president of the Fortune Group, an Atlanta-based corporation that markets business and professional development services. He is an expert on management, who once wrote a book about fatal errors that managers make. These include failure to develop people, failure to train people, attempting to manipulate people, and getting involved with the wrong people. To be a difference maker in business, Brown argued, the manager has to set standards and then build competence in the individuals who work for the organization. And there has to be a sensitive concern for people.[12]

This is the ServiceMaster policy. Maybe it should be a local church policy. It is a policy that puts emphasis on individuals and helps them to become more sensitive, compassionate, and caring.

Are some people innately more sensitive and caring than others? Probably. But we all can learn to be more aware of people and to be more sensitive. When you seek to be holy, to resist bitterness, and to keep yourself pure, you are better able to serve the Master as a people-sensitive difference maker. We must avoid the fatal error of allowing self-centered thoughts and actions to side-track us from our goals as difference makers who are sensitive to people. And as we increase in sensitivity, we will realize the importance of keeping a long-range perspective in our relationships and on life.

Principle Number Seven: Keep a Long-Range Perspective

Everybody knows that brothers don't always get along with one another, but the rivalry between Jacob and Esau started before they were even born. The Bible says they jostled with each other while they were still in the womb and it got no better as they grew up. Their interests and personalities were completely different, and their mother's tendency to play favorites probably didn't make things any better.

On several occasions the conflict reached life-changing proportions. Once Esau had been out hunting and came home famished. "Quick," he said to his younger brother, "let me have some of that red stew." Jacob was willing to hand over the meal, but first he wanted his brother to hand over the inheritance rights that came to a first born son. The hungry Esau agreed and gave away his future inheritance in exchange for a dish of meat.[13]

It didn't take long for Esau to recognize the foolishness of his short-term thinking, but by then it was too late.

Centuries after this happened, we can shake our heads in amazement at Esau's actions, but haven't we all been guilty of something similar? We get carried away with excitement or some other emotion and act in a way that we regret later. Perhaps that is why the writer of Hebrews reminded us that, "Esau . . . for a single meal sold his inheritance rights as the oldest son. Afterward, as you know, when he wanted to inherit this blessing, he was rejected."[14]

This has happened to some of our spiritual and political leaders who have fallen into short-term sexual liaisons without pondering the consequences until later. People get into long-term debt when they buy on "easy credit" without thinking about the bills that will come later. Car owners and home owners ignore some developing problem that is expensive to fix, and then face even higher repair bills. Business experts decry the practices of the many companies that are so concerned about the bottom line next quarter that they skimp on quality, set no funds aside for research, make no plans for the future, and then see their businesses fail. Sometimes we have the painful experience of watching others get into trouble because of short-term thinking: teenagers who experiment with drugs, students who drop out of school, an incompatible couple who gets married despite the advice of others who can see the negative long-term consequences.

Thinking ahead. Effective difference makers are not like Esau, who lived for the pleasures of the present and bartered away what God had prepared for the future. But neither are they day dreamers who don't accomplish much because their minds are so much in the future that they fail to take care of their present responsibilities. Effective difference makers see things from two perspectives. They work diligently in the present, and they keep their eyes on the future.

As we move toward the twenty-first century, a few innovative and forward-thinking people are watching present trends and making creative plans for the future. John Naisbitt, for example, is a trend watcher whose *Megatrends* books have become best sellers. Business journalist Joe Cappo welcomed the '90s with a fascinating book about trends that could shape the course of business throughout this decade and into the next century. Researcher George Barna has described how the future will change the face of the church. Another writer suggested that people with long-term vision need to develop what he called the Gretzky Factor. Wayne Gretzky, the best hockey player of his generation, has said that it's important to know where the puck is at any moment and where it will be going.[15]

Why do some hockey players seem to know where the puck is going? Why are some people able to write future trend books? Why does each field have a few trend-setters who have a finger on the pulse of where their businesses, professions, or societies seem to be headed? Is it possible that some individuals have a special feel for the future? Are there people who have rare abilities to make Gretzky-like guesses about what is coming and who have the courage to act accordingly? When these people are right about their predictions, they often reap great financial and political rewards. Frequently these trend-setters become significant difference makers.

But planning for the future and thinking ahead involve a lot more than subjective feeling. People who think ahead realistically almost always keep themselves informed. Innovators read widely and are knowledgeable about a broad range of current events, trends, issues, and thinking both within their fields and outside their areas of expertise.[16]

These people are known as visionaries, but their vision for the future comes because they know what is going on now. Sometimes they learn through their travels. They have a broad range of friends. They learn from adversity. They read the newspapers and they keep aware of the popular culture: trying to determine what others are watching on television and MTV, reading in magazines, or lining up to see at the movies.

Most of us who want to be difference makers don't have time to do all this information gathering. But we can keep our eyes and ears open and determine to never stop learning. In this way we develop a long-range perspective instead of retreating into narrow minded, self-absorbed, short-term thinking.

People who think ahead also make plans. When he reached his mid-eighties, comedian George Burns reportedly booked the London Palladium so he could perform there on his one-hundredth birthday. At age ninety, Armand Hammer said that he was limiting his long-range plans to only ten years because he wanted to see them happen. In his early nineties, Norman Vincent Peale was still thinking positively and making plans for the future. In contrast, we all know people who wake up each morning and have no plans beyond breakfast. These people are unlikely to be effective difference makers.

Knowing the future. We who are Christians have a perspective on the future that is different from the thinking of our non-Christian neighbors and coworkers. We believe that God created the universe, holds it together, knows what is happening here on earth, and has a plan for the future. Before his death and resurrection, Jesus told the disciples that he was going to prepare a place where believers would spend eternity, and he promised to come back and take us to be with him. He made it clear that nobody can predict the time of his return.[17]

A small portion of the Bible gives us glimpses of the events surrounding Christ's return and describes what will happen at the end of history. Much of this prophecy is written in figurative language that is difficult to understand. Because of this, serious, competent Bible scholars disagree about what biblical prophecies mean. Sadly, these disagreements have led to heated debates that have split churches, ruined friendships, and left people with lifelong animosity.

To complicate the picture, some individuals claim to have divine revelations that go beyond Scripture and give additional predictions about the future. A few months ago I was in Korea where a lady gave me a long letter describing a vision she had seen and asking if I could help her spread the message in America. People who claim to have these kinds of visions sometimes attract bands of devoted followers who are encouraged to quit their jobs, leave their families, and give away their possessions because of what the vision predicts. When some predicted event does not occur or when Christ does not reappear at the expected time, the leader claims that he or she misinterpreted the vision and tries again.

None of this is new. The New Testament church at Thessalonica was upset, alarmed, and probably confused by false prophecies and by misunderstandings of God's Word. Some believers apparently quit their jobs and were idly waiting for the Lord's return. Paul's two letters to the Thessalonians were efforts to correct such false thinking.

Christians believe that Christ will return, but we don't know when and can't be absolutely sure of the details. God holds the future, but this is no excuse for idleness, sloppy workmanship, or short-term thinking in the present.

I don't know to what degree Aurelia Rau thinks ahead, but she is a difference maker who has made rich investments in the future. Miss Rau is a short little lady, quiet and unassuming. She has gone to the same church for years and isn't noticed very much.

But my daughters know her, and they won't forget her. They had many dedicated Sunday school teachers when they were growing up, but Miss Rau was in a class by herself.

She has poured herself into the lives of the girls in her classes over the years, showing them love, supporting them with her prayers, sending them cards, and writing them notes of encouragement even after they have grown to adulthood.

Of all the difference makers in this book, perhaps none is shorter in height than Aurelia Rau. But from my perspective, none stands taller. Great will be her reward in the future—in heaven.

Chapter Highlights

- ‡ Christian difference makers seek to be holy, to be free of bitterness, to maintain purity, and to build up other people.
- ‡ Difference makers want to serve the Master. The most effective difference makers are compassionate and sensitive to others.
- ‡ The best difference makers work diligently in the present but are aware of the future. They have both an immediate and a long-range perspective.

10

Look for Ways
to Help Others

When I arrived at 7:30 in the morning, the air over Trivandrum was already saturated with humidity. Stepping from the air-conditioned comfort of the plane, I was engulfed by an oven-like blast of hot air that instantly brought beads of perspiration to my brow. Before I reached the terminal, droplets of moisture began to run down my back, wetting my shirt so it stuck to my sweating skin.

India is hot but fascinating: a kaleidoscope of brilliantly colored saris, swirling dust, majestic beauty, incredible poverty, lumbering oxcarts, fertile rice paddies, wandering cows, swarming people and swarms of flies, religious superstitions, curb-side fortune tellers, and pathetic beggars. No place captivates me more. This visit to the hot and humid city of Trivandrum, on the southern tip of the Indian subcontinent, was the last stop on a journey through several parts of the country.

My Indian hosts had agreed to meet me when the plane arrived, but because nobody was waiting, I assumed they had been delayed, perhaps by traffic. I lugged my bags to a bench in an alcove shielded from the sun, took a seat, and waited.

An hour passed.

Then two more hours passed, and three.

There was no air-conditioning in the waiting room and the oscillating fans on the ceiling brought little relief as the temperature rose. I went back outside in search of a breeze, but the air was still. The midday sun baked both the pavement and any living creature that ventured out from under the shade.

Had I been stranded in Los Angeles, Toronto, or Melbourne, I would have known what to do. A simple call or two from an air-conditioned phone booth would have brought the help I needed. Soon I would have been on my way.

But I didn't know whom to call in Trivandrum. I had no way of contacting anyone. All I could do was wait.

I spent the whole day in the airport and had to find a hotel after the airport closed. My Indian hosts had been misinformed about my arrival time and felt terrible after learning that I had sat in that sweltering terminal for over eleven hours.

I might still be there if it hadn't been for Mr. Ninan. He had noticed me during the day (as the only non-Indian in the small airport, I wasn't hard to spot), and like other airline employees, he wondered why I was waiting. When he heard that I had come to speak at a pastor's conference, his eyes brightened.

"I am not a Hindu," he said enthusiastically. "I am a Christian, like you, and I will find who was supposed to meet you."

And he did!

After the conference, I passed through the Trivandrum airport again, ready to leave on a flight to Bombay and then home. After looking for Mr. Ninan in the terminal, I spotted my helpful friend standing at the bottom of the stairs leading to the plane. While the other passengers went aboard and found their seats, I once again thanked Mr. Ninan for his overflowing kindness to a stranded stranger.

"Don't thank me for being kind," he said. "It's my duty."

Even now, several years later, I marvel at the gracious attitude of that man. I wrote a thank-you note after I got home and sent a little gift, but then we lost contact.

Probably he has long forgotten me, but I will never forget him. At a time when I needed help, Mr. Ninan was a difference maker.

He saw this as his duty.

If we want to change people's lives, we must also be alert to ways we can care for people. Hebrews 13 mentions three ways we can do this.

Principle Number Eight: Be a People Helper

Have you heard about YAVIS?

Several years ago, someone suggested that counselors like to work with YAVIS people: counselees who are *Y*oung, *A*ttractive, *V*erbal, *I*ntelligent, and *S*uccessful. These are the most pleasant people to be with. They are also the people who are least likely to come for counseling.

More often counselors work with people who are struggling, unattractive, and not able to put their problems into words. Beginning counselors may have visions of rescuing needy people, like knights in shining armor. Quickly, however, it becomes apparent that counseling is hard mental work that can be physically and emotionally draining. It isn't surprising that many professionals burn out after a few years and go into other work—like one of my friends who closed his counseling practice and moved to a tourist community where he opened a wine and cheese shop.

But there continue to be people who need help: the depressed, those who are anxious, the confused, people who have lost hope, couples with marriage difficulties or problems with their kids, substance abusers, individuals who struggle with their careers, victims of abuse, child molesters, and a host of others. When we are honest, most of us will admit the need for occasional help ourselves. The biblical instruction to bear one another's burdens must be taken seriously.[1]

The writer of Hebrews gives more specific directions: "Keep on loving each other as brothers. . . . Remember those in prison as if you were their fellow prisoners, and those who are mistreated as if you yourselves were suffering."[2]

Books on counseling almost always mention *empathy*. This comes from a German word that means to feel with someone. You may never have been in prison, but you can try to imagine what that experience would be like. You may never have been physically beaten, sexually abused, or ripped-off financially, but you can try to comprehend how you would feel if you had been ruthlessly victimized or mistreated. When we try to "feel with" people who are hurting, we are showing empathy. We are trying to understand the suffering of another person. Understanding and compassion often are what mistreated people most desperately need.

When I was in high school our church youth group would present services at the local rescue mission. I hated it.

The room was filled with unshaven, dirty men in worn, baggy clothes. Sometimes they smelled of urine and alcohol. Most showed little interest in our carefully planned evangelistic service. Often they would doze off until we were done; then they would shuffle away to get their free meal. My young mind did not think of "those who are mistreated as if you yourselves were suffering." In my youthful view these were drunks pulled from the gutters. I talked to a few of them, but I didn't show much empathy. I made little effort to learn about their lives. Looking back I am not proud of how I behaved toward those men.

Over the years I have begun, in small and limited ways, to glimpse the frustration, fears, and futility of people who are homeless. I have begun to sense what it means to be addicted to drugs and alcohol, without friends or food, and penniless. I have grown to appreciate the dedicated people who work in rescue missions with low pay and long hours. Often they have a thankless job. They may work for months to rehabilitate someone who falls back unexpectedly into a derelict lifestyle.

A few weeks before I began to write this book, I was invited to speak at the annual banquet of Union Gospel Ministries in Portland, Oregon. I accepted because a friend invited me, not because I had any desire to return to a rescue mission. My speech—at a nice suburban hotel and not in a soup kitchen—was warmly received, but I was the one who came away most changed.

For two days I toured the mission facilities, talked to the men and women who were being helped, met with the staff, and had lunch with some of the board members. I discovered that this inner-city work does much more than give shelter, meals, and clothing to the homeless. As in similar missions around the country, the people in Portland counsel unwed mothers, run a highly acclaimed, low-cost day-care center for working parents, and visit low-income elderly people who have limited mobility. They operate an evangelistic center for foreign sailors from visiting ships, run inner-city Bible clubs, offer a Christian recovery program for substance abusers, and fund much of their work by operating three thrift stores.

Of all their activities, the most amazing is Laurelwood Church. For many years this was a respected Presbyterian church with magnificent stained glass windows, beautifully carved wood, and an impressive pipe organ. The congregation had reluctantly relocated because there was no place for parking. So the mission took a church that had no parking and found a congregation that had no cars. They went to the homeless people of Portland and offered to bring them to a church specifically for them.

At first the attendance was small, but the pastor and his associates persisted. They resisted the urge to "just pull together a service for the street people" and determined, instead, to provide the best possible music and preaching. Every Sunday between two hundred and three hundred people now come to their church. There is Sunday school for the children, a separate program for Spanish-speaking people, and a choir composed of men who have been rescued from a hopeless lifestyle, even though many still live on the streets.

All of this is headed by a bright, caring young people helper named Don Michel. A few years ago he too was on the streets, a troubled teenager addicted to drugs. Then he was "cared for . . . told that God loved me and had a better plan for my life. It was what I had always looked for, someone to care, someone to care about me!"

Don Michel and his team members at Union Gospel Ministries are difference makers in large part because they have learned how to be people helpers.

How to be a people helper. How can we really help others? Entire books have been written on this subject, but a few basic principles are at the core of effective helping. You can practice these at home, at work, or anywhere else.

First, learn to show empathy. Try to imagine how others feel. If you can learn to see things from the other person's perspective, you will understand better and be more helpful.

Second, listen. Too often we rush to give advice, but we don't make the effort to listen carefully or to understand the situation. A few genuine questions like "what happened next" or "tell me more" will encourage a person to talk. You can make a significant difference in the lives of others if you listen earnestly and patiently, without condemning or rushing in with advice.

Third, make suggestions tentatively. Give the other

person a chance to respond and try not to be pushy or overbearing.

Fourth, be encouraging without being unrealistic. If someone has a terminal illness and knows it, don't promise that God will heal and that the problems will be gone by morning. God may indeed heal, but it also is possible that he will not. Be encouraging without making promises that may not come true.

Fifth, look for opportunities to talk about Christ. Don't force this or you could ruin your relationship and throw away a good opportunity to introduce someone to the Savior. Recognize that God helps us to determine both when and how to bring up spiritual issues. Often people need to know what God is really like. Some need to confess sins or need to hear about God's love and compassion.

Sixth, recognize that conversation is only one way to help. Tangible assistance such as food, clothing, or baby-sitting services can speak volumes about the love of Christ. When Prison Fellowship discovered how much prisoners worried about their families "on the outside," programs were started to address these concerns. Project Angel Tree, for example, gathers gifts, toys, and turkeys to distribute in the homes of prisoners whose families might otherwise have bleak Christmas celebrations.

In many communities there are prison ministries, rescue missions, places of refuge for battered women or abused children, half-way houses for former mental patients, shelters for the homeless, homes for the mentally retarded, day-care centers for the elderly, and other centers for young children. Most of these places are understaffed and welcome volunteers. If you want to be a difference maker and don't know where to start, try one of these facilities.

An unusual example. One of my favorite writers is a Dutch priest named Henri Nouwen. He has taught at both Harvard and Yale, and for nineteen years he served on the faculty at the University of Notre Dame. His books on spirituality have influenced Catholics and Protestants alike. When I was a seminary professor I urged all of my students to read at least one of Nouwen's books.

As he taught and wrote his books, however, Henri Nouwen sensed that his personal spiritual ambitions were different from what God wanted for his life. Often he prayed, "Lord, show me where you want me to go, and I will follow you," but he resisted "screaming and kicking" when he began to sense where God was leading. The new direction seemed clearly opposed to everything Nouwen had been trained for and was qualified to do.

Henri Nouwen, former professor, conference speaker, and giver of commencement addresses, now works at a community for handicapped people near Toronto. He lives in a house where the residents include a twenty-five-year-old man named Adam who does not speak, seldom smiles, and cannot let others know if he likes his food, wants something, or is hurting. Others don't know if Adam recognizes them. All his basic needs—dressing and undressing, walking, eating, going to the bathroom—need to be handled by somebody else. Often that somebody else is Henri Nouwen.

The former professor still writes and gives occasional lectures, but he is convinced that God wants him in the community where people like Adam live.[3]

Henri Nouwen is a people helper and a difference maker.

Principle Number Nine:
Show Hospitality

Shortly after our marriage, my wife and I left Oregon and moved to Minnesota where I had accepted a teaching position in a small liberal arts college. We rented an apartment and put away our wedding presents, but we had almost no furniture and very little money. We found a few odds and ends at garage sales and were able to transport them in our little Volkswagen, but our first home looked pretty empty. Our lives were filled with activities, but we didn't know many people apart from some colleagues at the college.

One of those colleagues was the registrar. He and his wife exuded warmth and gently entered our lives with friendship, love, encouragement, and genuine midwestern hospitality. We had meals in their home. They loaned us a few pieces of furniture until we could afford some of our own. When my wife, who is a nurse, had to work on our first Christmas Day, Paul and Faith Finlay delayed their traditional dinner plans so we could join them after work for a Christian celebration that we still remember. They lived in a modest home, but it always seemed to be open to students, visitors, and new arrivals at the college, like us.

Paul and Faith Finlay are difference makers.

In these days when even the smallest communities have comfortable motels with swimming pools, saunas, fancy restaurants, and low weekend rates, it is sobering to learn about inns in the ancient world. Apparently most were filthy, incredibly expensive, often dangerous, and of low repute. Running a brothel and keeping an inn were on about the same level.[4]

To help travelers avoid inns, people of the ancient world often opened their homes to provide hospitality. This was of special importance to the early Christians. Often they were treated with hostility in the heathen world where they lived. The high prices and low moral atmosphere discouraged believers from staying in the public inns.

So they stayed with one another, even if their hosts and hostesses were strangers to the guests. After writing about the past, present, and future of believers,[5] the author of the book of Hebrews reminded believers that they should "not forget to entertain strangers, for by so doing some people have entertained angels without knowing it."[6]

Surely the writer was thinking of those times in the Old Testament when visitors came as strangers, were entertained, and later were found to be angels.[7] In Bible times angels often appeared in human form, even though they normally are invisible. Sometimes the ancients recognized their visitors as angels; perhaps there were other times when angels came and their true identity wasn't revealed.

In a book about angels Billy Graham showed that these heavenly beings continue to serve as "God's secret agents." Hebrews 13:2 implies that angels might still appear as visitors. They look like humans but are really angels, and we don't even know it.

Today, strangers stay most often in motels, and our visitors are people whom we know: friends, relatives, neighbors, students, colleagues from work, fellow church members. When we open our homes to these people and welcome them, however, we are obeying a basic New Testament command to show and practice hospitality—without grumbling.[8]

Showing hospitality can be difficult. It isn't always easy to have guests in your home, especially if they stay too long or if they are demanding, inconsiderate visitors who are prone to criticize. We have some friends who once harbored a neighbor who was hiding from her husband. He had beaten her until her eyes were swollen shut and her face was black and blue. Such acts of hospitality can disrupt our schedules, cost money, and lead to spills on our carpets. Sometimes our valued possessions get broken.

But people who overlook the inconveniences, choosing instead to show hospitality, are difference makers.

I don't have to look far to see this. My wife, Julie, is a beautiful example of someone who has made a difference in many lives by showing hospitality. Over the years she has not forgotten to entertain strangers. Maybe she has entertained angels without knowing it.

Clearly her actions show another important difference-maker principle.

Principle Number Ten: Be a Marriage Builder

Almost everybody has heard about David and Bathsheba, but have you ever heard of David and Michal?

Michal was King Saul's daughter who fell in love with David. When the king learned about this he was tremendously pleased. David had become a threat to Saul, and the king reasoned that his own daughter could trap her new husband and arrange for his death. But when the soldiers came to carry out the murder, Michal helped David escape.

This could have been the start of a beautiful love story, but it wasn't. After David became king he once danced at the head of a great parade when the ark of the Lord was carried into Jerusalem. Michal watched from a window "and when she saw King David leaping and dancing before the Lord, she despised him in her heart." Later, in comments dripping with sarcasm, she expressed her feelings about the king. Her love was gone and so was their marriage. Michal was never heard of again.[9]

Like some biblical marriages, many marriages today are not happy. Current statistics tell us about high divorce rates, widespread spouse and child abuse, increasing numbers of unmarried couples who live together, astronomically high rates of illegitimate births, and the spread of pornography with its adverse effects on individuals and families. Many young people have never seen a good marriage. Books, movies, and television programs usually dwell on conflict, unfaithfulness, broken relationships, and passionate affairs outside of marriage. The writer of Hebrews seems strangely out of place writing that "marriage should be honored by all, and the marriage bed kept pure, for God will judge the adulterer and all the sexually immoral."[10]

When those words were written, society was even more adulterous and corrupt than ours is today, but Christians were remarkably unique. Galen, the Greek physician, was amazed when he wrote that believers "refrain from cohabiting all their lives." He added that Christians were "individuals who in ruling and controlling themselves, and in their keen pursuit of virtue, have attained a pitch not inferior to that of real philosophers." When Pliny the governor of Bithynis (in what is today Turkey) was sent to spy on Christians, the government was looking for reasons to bring charges against the young church. But in writing to the emperor, Pliny noted that the Christians had "bound themselves by an oath . . . to avoid theft or robbery or adultery, never to break their word, or repudiate a deposit when called upon to refund it." In the early church, believers lived with such a standard of purity that even their critics and enemies could find no fault.[11]

There are people like that today, people who have good marriages characterized by faithfulness, respect, compassion, companionship, and genuine love. Such marriages seem to be rare, however. Many of us find our marriages becoming weary relationships where there is boredom, routine living, shallow communication, and tired sex.

Several years ago, psychologist Kevin Leman wrote the book *Sex Begins in the Kitchen*.[12] With humor and illustrations from people's lives, Leman reminded readers that sexual intimacy starts long before a couple climbs into bed. Marriages remain healthy when a couple shows mutual consideration, genuine interest in one another's activities, a willingness to talk, and a determination to do things together that are fun. In good marriages, the husband and wife are honest about how they feel, willing to express compliments, and concerned enough to pray for one another. Authentic marriage, writes Bill Hybels, is a marriage where the husband and wife see their personality differences as blessings and not as reasons for conflict, where "spouses really feel loved. And where routine gives way to conversation, fun, and romance."[13]

If marriage is to be alive, pure, and fulfilling, there must be an unswerving commitment from both partners. When careers, hobbies, church activities, the demands of children, or daily schedules get in the way, the marriage begins to split.

Simple formulas cannot prevent divorce, but you can start protecting your marriage with a determination to keep your relationship alive. Back this up with time together, sharing, and creative efforts to do things together that are mutually enjoyable. Make up your mind to be faithful to your spouse, and avoid contacts and situations that could undermine your purity. Above all, undergird your marriage with daily prayer and get help if problems persist.

When marital tensions arise we often keep them to ourselves. If someone else is having family problems, most of us look the other way and say nothing. As a result, couples and families struggle alone. Everybody puts on a happy face and pretends that all is well when it isn't. As Christians we should pray for the marriages of others and do what we can to keep each other's families strong.

It is a great tragedy when people are difference makers in their communities, churches, and careers, but fail to make a positive difference at home.

Many years ago when our kids were small and we were living in the East, I met a distinguished Christian counselor who was an emerging leader in his field. The man had a genuinely charming wife, several children, and a successful private practice. He was active in his church, taught part-time at a local Christian college, and spoke periodically at national conferences.

As the years passed and his career grew, he got busier and busier. He was making a difference in many lives through his counseling and teaching, but his family was starting to unravel. When one of his kids began taking drugs, the father was too busy to meet with the school counselor. Instead he asked his wife to go alone. Other problems began to surface in the family, but this widely regarded Christian counselor was too involved with his career to be a difference maker at home.

You can guess what happened. The father spent increasing amounts of time at the office. He found it more fulfilling to be with admiring patients and stimulating professional colleagues than to be at home with his disintegrating family. The counselor began to discuss his problems with one of his female patients. This lady, he said, understood him better than his wife. Soon his family and marriage fell apart. His competence as a counselor began to slip and his career came to a grinding halt. He married the understanding lady, but that marriage didn't last long.

When I saw him recently, he smiled as if nothing had happened and told me about his counseling practice. He is involved in a little church and knows that God has forgiven him. He is looking for new opportunities to help people, but he has left behind a trail of wounded counselees, colleagues, and family members. When we sacrifice our families in a quest to change the world or to reach the top, we end up not making much of a lasting difference at all.

Chapter Highlights

‡ If you want to be a difference maker, make every effort to be a people helper.
‡ People helpers show empathy—the ability to feel with others and to see things from their perspectives.
‡ To be a people helper, learn to show empathy, listen carefully, make suggestions tentatively, be encourag-

ing (without being unrealistic), look for opportunities to talk about Christ, and recognize that talking is only one way to help. We can also help by giving tangible assistance.

‡ Difference makers show hospitality without complaining despite the inconveniences.

‡ To be a difference maker, make every effort to build marriages—your own and the marriages of others.

11

Manage Your Resources

Every evening a radio personality in the Chicago area closes his program with the same six powerful words: "Take it easy, but take it!"

I can't think of a more accurate summary of the philosophy of this age: Take what you can get. Accumulate possessions. Reach for the top. Push for more money. Expect that God will make you rich. Grab all the gusto you can get. The best way to die is to die shopping! The happiest man is the man with the most toys.

The message is hard to resist. We know that the love of money is at the root of all kinds of evil. We have read Jesus' statement that nobody can serve both God and money. We know that wealth is no assurance of God's blessing, and we have heard the sad story of the rich young man who refused to follow Jesus because it would mean giving up his wealth and possessions.[1] Some of us have heard that the Bible has about 450 references to money and that Jesus talked more often about money than about the combined subjects of heaven, hell, sexual immorality, and violence.

Still, most of us have a deeply ingrained itch for just a little more. Our minds come up with all kinds of reasons for spending money we don't have, using easy credit, or getting just one or two more things before we declare ourselves content with life.

"Don't say that getting money isn't important or that it isn't good to be rich," a friend said recently. "The more you have, the more you can contribute to worthy causes. What if

God wants you to be rich? And in any case, people should pay you for what you're worth."

Reasoning like this can be hard to resist. Won't we be more effective in helping others if we have more to give? Couldn't my wife and I be more hospitable if we had a house that was just a little bigger and a bit nicer than the one we have? Wouldn't we have more opportunities to touch lives if we didn't have to spend time worrying about money? Surely our churches and Christian colleges could have a greater impact if they had larger budgets, bigger television ministries, better buildings, or nicer campuses. Wouldn't it be good to stretch our faith by making purchases beyond our means and then trusting God to provide the extra money? All of these are rationalizations that entice us to pursue wealth while keeping us deep in debt.

Principle Number Eleven:
Be Content With What You Have

Several years ago, in a powerful article about learning to live with money, Philip Yancey wrote about his friends who had done well financially. "In most cases, a large home and fine furniture make them less hospitable, not more. Our conversations, which had once ranged over personal and social concerns, kept drifting to comparisons of clothing labels, gourmet restaurants, and video recorders. Affluence had a strangely distancing effect. It created barriers."[2]

In contrast, the writer of Hebrews presents a message that is hard to swallow. "Keep your lives free from the love of money and be content with what you have."[3]

It is much easier to be a difference maker when you are not worried about money or weighed down by debt.

Bill Russell learned that lesson just in time. As a bright young lawyer with a dynamic law firm in Seattle, he was on the fast track to a significant and lucrative career. One day,

Bill was in a car with his boss when the older man decided to stop briefly to see how construction was progressing on his third house. Clearly, this was not going to be a cottage; it looked more like a palatial mansion.

The young lawyer was very impressed and commented on his employer's career accomplishments.

"To tell you the truth," the older man said wistfully as they stood watching the construction workers, "I hate this place. I don't need it even though I can well afford it. Everybody knows that I have been successful in my career. I have all the money I need, and more. But I don't have any friends. I'm divorced with two ex-wives. I have three children and they all hate me."

Bill listened as his boss went on to talk about the future.

"I want to prepare you, Bill, to take over the business. When I'm gone, all I have will be yours."

Suddenly the young lawyer was gripped by a disturbing thought. This was an incredible opportunity that would give him power and riches, but there would be a terrible price. "If I have all this and get to where my employer is," Bill thought to himself, "I will be like him."

Several months later, Bill became a Christian and mentioned this to his boss. The reaction was immediate and decisive: "You cannot be a Christian and be successful in this practice! Either you leave that Christianity or you leave this firm." Bill was given two weeks to make his decision.

It didn't take that long. Bill Russell quit his job, cleaned out his desk, and has never looked back.

Today he works for a mission. He has far less money than he could have had and he lives in a modest house. But he has peace of mind and inner contentment. In a quiet and unassuming way, Bill Russell is a difference maker.

Three modern traps. Several years ago, Richard Foster wrote a powerful and insightful book in which he described three seductive forces that have pulled at individuals throughout history. "Virtually every major thinker and every great movement have wrestled with these issues," Foster wrote.[4] "No issues touch us more profoundly or universally. No topics cause more controversy. . . . No three things have been more sought after or are more in need of a Christian response." These are the topics that Satan most uses to manipulate and ensnare unsuspecting human beings. They are forces that have led to abuse and corruption throughout history. They have destroyed unsuspecting families, clever journalists, successful Wall Street tycoons, savvy politicians, promising careers, and prominent Christian ministries. In themselves, these forces are not bad, but when misused, they can control our thinking and devastate our lives. If we fail to control them, these forces will control us.

The three potential villains are money, sex, and power. These were so dangerous that the ancient monastics took vows of poverty, chastity, and obedience to get free of them. At other places in this book, we consider sex and power. In the remainder of this chapter we will focus on money.

How we allow money to affect us and what we do with it determines, in large measure, whether or not we become effective difference makers. In themselves riches are not wrong. Wealthy people like Abraham or Solomon have been used by God throughout history. By giving away money modern philanthropists make a great difference in the lives of many others. Small gifts from millions of people have kept churches and missions alive and have helped the victims of earthquakes and famines. Similar contributions have built hospitals, created schools, and sent inner-city kids to camp. Thousands of concerned people regularly contribute to provide shelter for homeless people whom they have never met.

Still it is hard to keep our lives free from the love of money.[5] We live in an affluent society where compulsive extravagance has become an addiction. Even the church has accepted the lies that more is better and that we should expect God to make us rich.

How do we avoid the lust for money and keep from getting entangled with worries about finances? The answers aren't easy, but here are some guidelines.

First, never forget God's nearness. When the checkbook is overdrawn and bills pile up, he often seems silent and far away. At those times (most of us have been there) it is hard to concentrate on helping others or to think about anything beyond meeting our own needs. But God doesn't leave us or forsake us. That is a clear message in Hebrews: "We can say with confidence, The Lord is my helper."[6] He can help us hang on to this attitude, especially when we are inclined to doubt or forget.

Second, be content with what you have. This goes against our whole way of thinking. From childhood, we are taught to strive for more: more success, more security, more possessions, more prestige, more accomplishments, more friends, more money. Contentment sounds dangerous. We fear it is an excuse for laziness or that it limits our vision and ambition.

The Bible never condones laziness, lack of vision, or poor planning. But neither does it sanction the competitive drive for possessions, prominence, and power that is the mark of our age.

Contentment is a mental attitude. There is only one effective way to learn it: let your thoughts be filled with thanksgiving. With God's help, we can discipline ourselves to stop yearning for things we don't have and start thanking him for what we do have. We can turn from frustrated longing to gratitude. Thanksgiving does not destroy ambition; it redirects our ambition. When we are continually aware of God's provisions for us, the focus of our ambition shifts from meeting our own needs to serving the Lord by serving others. This is radical thinking, but it is also biblical thinking. In lives of service, thanksgiving and contentment strengthen one another.

Too often we treat God like a genie in the sky who exists to fulfill our wishes. Our prayers are filled with requests for things. We approach God with a shopping list, beg for what we want, and give only passing thought to his greatness, goodness, holiness, sovereignty, and past provisions.

The Scriptures certainly instruct us to bring our requests to God, but these must be accompanied by thanksgiving. Then God is pleased and our anxieties—including worries over money—are replaced with a sense of peace.[7]

Third, try to manage your money well. Slipshod financial management is a foolish and irresponsible misuse of what God has given. If you have trouble managing money, find someone who can give you financial guidance.

Fourth, become a giver. The rich young man whom we mentioned earlier was unwilling to part with his possessions so he turned from Jesus and walked away sorrowfully. In contrast Jesus once watched a poor widow give all she had. Her contribution was small, but her willingness to give was enormous. That willingness, the Scriptures tell us, is far more important than the size of the gift.[8]

The world is filled with people who want our money. Almost every week I get several letters asking for a contribution. Most of the appeals are convincing and the causes are worthy. I want to give liberally and without strings attached, but I also want to give carefully. None of us can give to everyone who asks, and deciding where to send our money is sometimes difficult.

A set of personal guidelines for giving can help us with these decisions. Usually I give to my church or to other organizations that have demonstrated their ability to handle contributions responsibly and wisely. I rarely respond to emotional appeals or to panicky letters, and I almost never give to individuals who write with requests for gifts or handouts.

I agree with Richard Foster, however, that "there are times when we need to throw caution to the winds and give, just give. We need to risk giving to individuals, not because they have proven that they can handle money well, but because they need it. In so doing, we give love and trust as well. And we free ourselves from that clutching, money-loving spirit that spells spiritual ruin."[9]

If you want to be a difference maker, be a giver.

Becoming a Giver

Jane Edna Hill was a giver. She didn't always give money; often her pastor-husband's salary didn't leave many dollars to give. But Jane Hill (whom everyone called "Baby") gave love, encouragement, and acceptance. Sometimes she surprised people with her courage.

Every Thursday morning she was among the volunteers serving breakfast at The Lord's Kitchen, a center for transients and homeless people. Each visitor was treated courteously, but sometimes the guests weren't very cooperative.

One morning a huge, middle-aged lady appeared and quickly dominated the whole dining room. "I'm Pippi Longstocking," she bellowed when somebody asked her name. Her face was dirty and scarred, her clothes were torn, and she radiated belligerence.

On her second visit, the woman announced that her name was Snow White. On day three she was Ronald Reagan and on the fourth day, the day when Baby was on duty, the woman growled, "I'm Jesus Christ. Don't mess with me!"

But Jane Hill was not easily intimidated. "Listen, sweetheart," she said. "Your name isn't Jesus Christ. I happen to know that man personally and he doesn't look anything like you."

The room suddenly grew silent. Everybody stopped to see what would happen next. The woman clenched her callused hands into fists and glared with anger.

"These people may think you're mean or dangerous," the pastor's wife continued, "But I know you're not. You're angry. Life has been unfair to you. But you're not the only person suffering in this place. So why don't you wipe that frown off your face, use this towel to wash yourself in the bathroom, and come back here and sit beside me. I'll pour us an extra cup of coffee and we'll talk."

Suddenly the tough-looking woman collapsed in tears. "My name is Elizabeth," she said softly.

"My name is Jane," Baby answered as she gave her new friend a hug. And the whole room—cooks, dishwashers, volunteers, patrons—applauded.

In the weeks that followed, Elizabeth and Jane had coffee every Thursday morning in The Lord's Kitchen. Jane never said what they talked about, but the scowl on Elizabeth's face gave way to frequent smiles.

Maybe Elizabeth was among the three thousand mourners who came to the church a few months later on the day of Jane's funeral. Her husband, the Rev. Edward Victor Hill—one of this country's most-respected preachers—sat on the platform of his Los Angeles church and looked into the faces of the people who crowded the pews. Many had been touched and permanently changed by Baby's giving, caring spirit.[10]

I never met Mrs. Hill; I wish I had. Her life was an example of what this book is all about. She was a giver who had learned to be content with what she had.

Jane Edna Hill was a difference maker.

Chapter Highlights

‡ Difference makers learn to be content with what they have. They try to keep out of debt and they learn to give joyfully. It is hard to be a difference maker if you are worrying about unpaid bills or if your mind is set on accumulating as much as you can get.

‡ Pursuing money, sex, and power hinders our effectiveness as difference makers.

‡ To keep from being trapped by the love of money, never forget God's nearness, learn to be content with what you have, try to manage your money wisely, and become a cheerful giver. It is then that you will be a strong difference maker.

12

Select Good Mentors

*D*allas *had never seen anything like it.*

The people lined the streets, in some places six or seven deep, and crowded into the city hall plaza. Television cameras were set up in strategic locations and satellite transmissions were beamed worldwide. Mexican and Canadian publications, the British News Service, *USA Today*, and publications from all over the country had reporters on the scene. Telegrams were waiting from Billy Graham, from the president of the United States, and from admirers around the world.

The crowd was festive. Many held banners, signs, and posters. People stood on the roofs of their cars, climbed on top of newspaper boxes, or leaned out of office windows along the parade route. A lady in a wheelchair was pushed to the edge of the sidewalk where she could see better. Fathers stood in the warm spring sunshine holding little kids on their shoulders.

Slowly the color guards, the bands, the clowns, the Shriners (grown men riding go-carts and waving to the crowds) all passed by. There were convertibles, celebrities, and eighty-six floats.

But the loudest cheers were saved for the man in the straw fedora and light blue sports coat who rode with his wife at the end of the parade in a vintage, blue 1954 Buick Skylark. Smiling and waving to the crowd was the man whom all of Dallas had grown to love.

Tom Landry, coach of the Dallas Cowboys.

Technically, Tom Landry was no longer the coach when

he rode toward City Hall on that April morning. A few days before this festive parade Landry had been fired, abruptly and without warning. Now a grateful city, still reeling from shock and anger over the way this gentle man had been treated, had come out to show its affection.

Tom Landry had been disappointed, angry, and hurt when he lost his job so suddenly, but he responded with characteristic dignity and gentleness. Never a man to hide his deep faith in Jesus Christ, Landry knew then—as he knows now—that his life was in God's hands. His own pastor was deeply bothered by events surrounding the coach's firing, but it was Landry who put things into perspective. "It's all right," he said to his pastor. "I'm not worried about it, really, because God has something else planned for me."

Football star Herschel Walker summed up what many must have felt. "What made him the legend he is today is the excellent role model he was for the people. Coach Landry was a consistent, concerned citizen who realized the value of displaying a clean image. . . . I looked up to him for his Christian beliefs. He stood solid on that."[1]

Few people ever get parades and city hall receptions in their honor. Most of us are never mentioned in the evening news, and we don't get our names in the newspapers, except in an obituary notice. Few of us understand the intricacies of American football and a lot of people wonder if it makes any sense for grown men to bash into each other, breaking bones and straining muscles in the presence of wildly cheering crowds every Sunday afternoon in the fall. It isn't easy for us to identify with Tom Landry, whose whole life and work were so much related to football and whose example was so lauded on that spring day in Dallas. He seems so different from the rest of us. But Landry's example suggests another difference-maker principle that can apply to us all.

Principle Number Twelve:
Learn from Those Who are Leaders

Throughout our lives, we are indirectly influenced by prominent people like Tom Landry. Much more often, however, we are directly touched by people who are less famous. According to the Bible, the best examples for us are people who speak openly about their faith and who have exemplary lifestyles. The writer of Hebrews established these standards as a personal goal. He or she wanted a clear conscience and a life that was honorable in every way, so others could imitate it safely.[2] If you want to be a difference maker strive to imitate those who are examples to others. Seek to be an example whom others might want to follow.

Most of this we can accept without difficulty. We gladly *look* for difference makers who are good models and we would like to *be* difference makers who can be examples to others. But we are less enthusiastic about the biblical instruction to "obey your leaders and submit to their authority. They keep watch over you as men who must give an account. Obey them so that their work will be a joy, not a burden, for that would be of no advantage to you."[3] Voluntarily following somebody else's good example is one thing. Submitting to others and being held accountable is an entirely different matter.

But difference makers for God rarely serve in isolation. Effective difference makers are accountable to others.

The Old Testament writer of Ecclesiastes (probably King Solomon) wrote that "two are better than one, because they have a good return for their work: If one falls down, his friend can help him up. But pity the man who falls and has no one to help him up!"[4] A similar message appears in Proverbs 27:17: "As iron sharpens iron, so one man sharpens another."

Intellectually we accept our need for one another, but in our careers and daily living we are more inclined to act alone. That's the American (and Canadian) way. We are great believers in individual rights and admire people who seem to make a difference without help. We resist the "meddling" of others when they hold us accountable.

Nevertheless, writes Ted Engstrom, "an unaccountable spouse is living on the edge of risk; an unaccountable CEO is in danger of taking his company down a wrong road; an unaccountable pastor has too much authority; an unaccountable counselor has too much responsibility and needs too much wisdom to be able to handle it on his own."[5]

To whom are you accountable—really accountable—for your attitudes, your work, your worship, your goals, your personal and spiritual life? I asked a young pastor that question recently and he pointed upward to God and then to himself. This kind of independence from others allows dedicated people to make unwise decisions, to fall into sin or error, and sometimes to undermine all of their previous efforts to be difference makers.

This happened to one of my former students. He had done well in seminary and appeared to be launched into a fruitful ministry. The little church that he started was having an influence. Lives were being changed and people were coming to Christ. The pastor was a powerful and magnetic speaker whose enthusiasm and youthful attractiveness drew people to his church.

But he was living a double life and nobody knew—not his wife, his church board, his best friends, or even the woman with whom he was secretly having an affair. When the truth became known his whole ministry disintegrated.

One of his seminary classmates summed up the tragedy: "He made a tremendous difference in a lot of lives, but now many have become disillusioned with the faith that he shared and the Christ whom he preached. God is willing and able to forgive him, of course. But all the good that was accomplished is buried under the massive pile of harm that has come to the lives that have been hurt because of his immorality."

Many Christians live life as a solo act. We need others, of course, and we like being with others. But we have learned to handle things by ourselves. We pass exams, build credit, earn money, develop careers, make plans, and seek to grow spiritually pretty much on our own. When temptations, crises, or failures come, we are still on our own. When we most need others, we find that few people are there to forgive, encourage, support, or hold us accountable.

Corporations have boards of directors and churches have elders, but powerful CEOs or pastors can sometimes control their boards and get what they want. Most of us fail to notice when individuals begin to become self-promoted, power-wielding superstars.

When prominent people fall into sin or break the law, their actions usually flow from lives that have no real accountability. A strong individual or a small group of like-minded people has become accustomed to making decisions alone. They are not responsible to anybody. When they fall there is no one to lift them up. When they make an unwise decision, they have nobody to blame but themselves. The landscape of history is dotted with people and organizations that could have had a tremendous impact for good, but instead did incredible harm. They all had a similar theme song: "I'll do it my way!"

I have a good friend who recently sent me a note about accountability. "I've learned that it's not enough to just wish people would hold you accountable," he wrote. "I used to talk about accountability, teach accountability, and praise the merits of accountability. Then one day I realized that I had very little of it in my own life. It occurred to me that if it was really going to happen, I would have to ask for it."

This can be risky. Sometimes the people you ask are too busy or unwilling to hold you accountable. But my friend took the risk. He approached two mature brothers in Christ and suggested that they meet on a regular basis to encourage and check up with one another to make sure they are living the lives that they profess. The effectiveness of that group has increased as the little threesome has grown in mutual trust and vulnerability. But this didn't happen until my friend took the risk of asking others for their input.

The New Testament epistles record over fifty "one another" passages. Christians are told, for example, to love one another, build up one another, encourage one another, care for one another, and be kind to one another. Difference making is a two way street. It isn't very effective when one person is doing most of the giving with little mutual sharing and accountability. Difference makers need and depend on one another.

A few weeks before I started work on this book, I met with a group of believers and presented some of the material that I planned to include in these pages. I asked for reactions and shortly afterwards got a thoughtful letter.

"Many Christians are disillusioned about the fact that the church in this country often seems to have so little impact upon its members," the letter began. "Most studies indicate that there is little or no difference between Christians and the world in divorce rate, abortion rate, premarital sex, financial management, selection of TV and movie entertainment, etc. Yet many Christians make all sorts of claims about how Jesus has made a difference in their lives."

That letter got me thinking. Why do we proclaim that Christ has made a difference when, for many of us, being a Christian doesn't make much practical difference at all? Why have Christians, especially evangelicals, become the target of media jokes and sarcastic comments that mock our claims of personal transformation? Why do sophisticated yuppies and educated suburbanites ignore the age-old message of the Gospel while going out on a limb to follow the new-age teachings about harmonic convergence, crystal consciousness, out-of-body experiences, universal energy, karma, spirit guides, mantras, and pyramid power? How can vague concepts and equally vague answers give any real help to people searching for authentic spirituality? Why do millions of people claim to follow Christ and attend church regularly, but come away untouched and unchanged? Why do we call Christianity the Good News while attending church services where we never expect to hear anything either new or good?

We live in communities surrounded by empty, shallow people who are looking for something genuine to fill the void in their lives. Too often we offer them boredom, irrelevance, slick productions, appeals for money, and lives that aren't changed by the Word of God. My letter-writing friend has a point: for many Christians the Gospel doesn't make much difference in their daily lives, and neither does the church.

Some churches offer a weekly spiritual high with a good show that emphasizes enthusiasm while making few demands for obedience or calls for silent worship before a holy God. Other churches stress rules, proper behavior, and the need for aggressive evangelism or social outreach. There are many activities, but little emphasis is placed on compassion, forgiveness, or knowing God personally. Still other churches give scholarly lectures and emphasize correct doctrines. Their congregations are filled with people who have sharp minds but dull, cold hearts. They are what Flora Wuelluer, author of *Prayer and the Living Christ*, called "an organization of well-meaning idealists, working for Christ but far from his presence and power." Few of our churches emphasize genuine personal spirituality based on a commitment to spiritual discipline. Most fail to combine sacrificial service with solid biblical teaching and consistent worship.[6] Few call for genuine commitment and accountability.

I write this not to point a finger, but to point to a sad situation that affects us all—and for which we all must bear some of the blame. Glandion Carney has written about the Christians he knows "whose spirituality has simply faded away. Their growth dead-ended in sluggishness and inertia. At one time they possessed a vibrant love for God, almost euphoric and all-consuming. But somehow it ground to a halt."[7]

Carney is reluctant to judge these people because anyone can be trapped by the demands of work, family, and other obligations. At times we all feel like giving up. Dedicated pastors get tired and discouraged trying to instill spiritual vitality in resistant pew warmers who refuse to change. Dedicated laypeople get frustrated when church leaders lose their first love and become distracted by numbers, programs, fund raising, and church politics.

How can we rekindle the fires of renewal and develop a genuine hunger for righteousness and spiritual maturity? The answer is balance.

Strength in balance. My friend Devlin plays golf on occasion but isn't as successful as he would like. I can understand his problem. I abandoned the game years ago when my little white ball never seemed to go where I intended! My friend, in contrast, has persisted despite the frustrations. On a recent visit to the golf course, Devlin was having trouble keeping the ball on the fairway.

"I think I can see your problem," a fellow golfer commented. "Your feet aren't in the right position. So you lose your balance a little each time you swing the club. This causes the ball to veer to the side. If you keep your balance, you will have greater strength. Always remember, 'there is strength in balance.'"[8]

In all of life there is strength in balance. This is certainly true in our spiritual lives. We need to balance *private* times of conversation with God, Bible study, solitude, and meditation, and *public* times of learning from the Word of God, prayer, interaction with other believers, and partaking of the sacraments.[9] There must be balance between personal spiritual growth and practical Christian service to others. We need balance between rejoicing with those who rejoice and weeping with those who weep. We need to see God's hand, both in his bountiful provisions and in the suffering and persecution he permits so we can grow.

When we get off balance or follow leaders whose lives are unbalanced, we are less able to be difference makers.

Your personal board of directors. Late in his life, King David decided to take a census of his troops. This was a massive undertaking and there was no clear reason for all the effort. Apparently David was proud of all the troops that were under his command and curious about how many he really had.

The king didn't consult anybody about this. He simply issued an order that the census be taken. When Joab, chief of the army, questioned the wisdom of this decision, David overruled him. The complicated process took almost ten months, all to support David's ego. No wonder God was displeased.

After Joab reported the results of the count, the king realized that he had been wrong and was overwhelmed with guilt.[10] The entire incident would have been prevented if David had listened to his advisors.

What was true for David centuries ago applies to businesses, corporations, academic institutions, churches, and governments today. When people act without the advice of others, they risk making grave errors that lead to guilt, disappointment, and even chaos. Wise decisions are much more likely when a leader is surrounded by trusted advisors who are not afraid to ask questions, challenge plans, and give counsel.[11] The best leaders know that independent decisions can be dangerous.

What about believers who want to serve Christ by making a difference in the lives of others? Should you and I have our own personal boards of directors? At times we all need people who can help us make decisions, handle financial crises, or work through personal problems. Sometimes we go to a professional for help, but more often we go to a trusted friend, relative, or colleague. Many of us who are married are accountable to our spouses. Some find accountability in a Bible study or self-help group.

Getting advice is important, but most people also need help in keeping commitments. Have you ever gone on a diet, started an exercise program, decided to return to school, made up your mind to study harder, or begun a daily quiet time with God and given up shortly after you got started? Being accountable to another human being can make a great difference in your motivation.

Several months ago, I decided to look for a personal board of directors, a group of people who could oversee my work activities and hold me accountable. I prayed about this carefully, my wife and I discussed it at length, and eventually I asked some people if they would be willing to serve on this informal advisory board.

One of the people I approached was a pastor. "I will be on your board," he told me after a time of prayerful deliberation, "but only if you are willing to submit to us in your personal and spiritual life as well as in your professional life." My friend wanted to hold me completely accountable. He knows that we all need this if we are to be consistent difference makers. I agreed to his condition.

Principle Number 13:
Select Your Teachers Carefully

Mark Hennebach is an unusual teacher. Ask any of his 7th grade students at Howe Elementary School.

Every summer, usually in August before school opens,

Mr. Hennebach makes his way to each of the homes where the members of his fall class live. He carries a letter of introduction, written and signed by his students from the year before.

"Dear New Students," a recent letter began. "We, the undersigned, have spent a year with Mr. Hennebach. Here's what we want you to know about him. We wish we had known these things in September!"

There is nothing boring or conventional about Mark Hennebach's teaching. The school principal calls him creative, unusual, selfless, and humble. When he won a one-thousand-dollar award for exemplary teaching, he used it to buy software for the computer in his classroom. He trains student tutors and then pays them two dollars an hour to help younger kids who are having academic difficulties. He pays for a phone on his desk, so he can be in touch with parents at all hours of the school day. On weekends he drives kids to the Ala-Teen meetings that help teenagers with alcoholic relatives. Sometimes he pays for summer camp when students want to go but can't afford it.

Why does a man in his mid-thirties do all of this?

With the blessing of his family and the support of his suburban local church, Mark Hennebach, who is white, moved into a mostly black community so he could relate better to his students. He cares nothing about amassing wealth or being famous. According to an article in the *Chicago Tribune*, the teacher's altruism "springs from a deep religious faith, an evangelical calling that has driven him" throughout his adult life.[12]

"I know that I am living where I'm supposed to be living, working where I'm supposed to be working, and doing what I'm supposed to be doing," he told a reporter. He doesn't violate school rules about separation of church and state, but he sees himself as a missionary to the twelve- and thirteen-year-old inner-city kids at Howe Elementary

School. Three words hang in red letters across the front of his classroom. They guide his activities and are impressed on the minds of his students. Those words are *gratitude, honesty*, and *trust*.

Mark Hennebach is an unusual teacher. "He marches to a different drummer," says the principal, "but it's a nice beat."

Clearly Mark Hennebach is a difference maker. In his seventh grade classroom, he is a model for his students as well as an exemplary teacher of basic academic subjects.

But not all teachers are like that, and it is for this reason that our choice of teachers is just as important as the quality of our leaders. The writer of Hebrews warned us to examine our teachers carefully. "Do not be carried away by all kinds of strange teachings," we read.[13] The Bible establishes high standards for teachers. "Not many of you should presume to be teachers," warns James 3:1. "We who teach will be judged more strictly."

A good teacher like Mark Hennebach can make a powerful difference for good in the lives of his students. "He's the best teacher I ever had," said one twelve-year-old. "He teaches us things I didn't think we'd learn. He helps us with geometry. I'm starting to like geometry. I used to hate it." In contrast, a poor teacher can destroy student interest, creativity, motivation to learn, or self-esteem.

Watch out for strange teachings. Think about your teachers. Some probably made a lasting impact for good. Others may have left scars that still cause you pain. Even worse, religious teachers can damage the spiritual lives of people by leading them into great theological error. Jeremiah and Ezekiel were among the Old Testament prophets who boldly proclaimed the truth that came from God. They were surrounded by false teachers who told the people what they wanted to hear. The people of Israel ignored God's true teachers, listened to the false prophets, and faced destruction and death because of their choices.

In his last letter, Paul warned Timothy about the future and gave instructions that must be taken seriously by any Christian teacher. "Preach the Word; be prepared in season and out of season; correct, rebuke and encourage—with great patience and careful instruction. For the time will come when men will not put up with sound doctrine. Instead, to suit their own desires, they will gather around them a great number of teachers to say what their itching ears want to hear. They will turn their ears away from the truth and turn aside to myths. But you, keep your head in all situations.[14]

In one sense all of us are teachers, even if we never stand in front of a class. Parents are teachers. Employers are teachers. People in the media are teachers. All of us have a responsibility to be careful what we pass on to others.

But all of us are also students. Like Timothy, we need to "keep our heads" and make sure our thinking is clear in a time when we are surrounded by all kinds of strange teachings. Some of the current new age ideas sound enticing and convincing, but they often originate in a Christ-less eastern mysticism. Some strange teaching comes from professors, social critics, authors of self-help books, or the writers of popular songs and television sitcoms. Sometimes the teaching comes from preachers who may not even be aware of how far their heretical ideas deviate from biblical truth.[15]

If we are not cautious, any of us can be "carried away by all kinds of strange teachers." When that happens, it is difficult to influence people for good.

Evaluate what your teachers say. Over the years, I have met people who are experts in uncovering theological error. They are skilled at pointing out the weaknesses in false arguments that sound convincing. Filled with knowledge about the Bible and aware of the principles of logic, these Christians can spot heresy and logical contradictions that the rest of us wouldn't notice. When cultists, atheists, and others raise difficult questions, write articles, or speak in debates, my friends are able to give carefully reasoned and convincing answers. Sometimes they write books to help the rest of us guard against deceptive teachers, but a lot of the books are dull and difficult for non-experts to understand.[16]

Most of us cannot spend hours studying the Scriptures and understanding heresy. There are some ways, however, by which we can all avoid the errors and persuasive arguments of false teachers:

‡ Find out about the teacher's training and credentials. You can learn a lot by knowing where the teacher works or was trained, who publishes his or her books, and who is sponsoring the teacher's lectures. Be especially cautious of people who keep their backgrounds, training, and affiliations hidden or vague.

‡ Look at who the teacher quotes and how the quotations are handled. Be especially careful to look at the way the Bible is used. Many years ago a psychologist named O. Hobart Mowrer argued that the early church was able to help people because the members confessed their faults to one another. Mowrer quoted James 5:16 to prove his case, but he only used part of the verse and he ignored its context. James was writing about prayer, but Mowrer never mentioned that because he didn't believe in praying to a personal God. Be careful of people who take Bible verses or quotations from others out of context.

‡ Be cautious of those who continually emphasize one part of Scripture (such as healing, evangelism, prophecy, love, the Holy Spirit, or divine judgment) but overlook or rarely mention the rest. Good Bible

teaching is always balanced. Good Bible teachers don't conveniently ignore parts of the Bible.

‡ Be wary when anyone makes sweeping statements. A psychiatrist friend once told me that "all charismatics are hysterical." This was a sweeping statement that has no validity. Researchers have not demonstrated any differences in degree of stability between charismatic Christians and those who are not charismatic. People who make sweeping statements often are expressing strong, personal opinions that ignore important, documented facts.

‡ Watch how a teacher responds to criticism. We all get defensive at times, but when a teacher won't listen to criticism or evaluate contradicting evidence, he or she may be rigid, close-minded, and wrong.

‡ Look at the teacher's students. Jesus warned against false teachers who look good and sound good. Some make prophetic statements, drive out demons, and perform miracles, but they don't know Christ personally. You can always recognize a tree by its fruit, Jesus stated. In a similar way, we often can recognize false teaching by the actions and attitudes of those who are taught. False teachers do not produce godly individuals whose lives show the fruit of the Spirit.[17]

‡ Get help from individuals or authors you can trust. After listening to a few sermons, you can begin to discern whether your pastor is informed enough to give you guidance. Sometimes a reputable bookstore manager can recommend a book or author whose ideas can be trusted. Look around and you will find knowledgeable Christians who are dependable and able to give you guidance in making good decisions.

‡ Be a consistent Bible student. In one of their books, cult experts Bob and Gretchen Passantino tell about a young man named Joe who came to work as their staff

intern. From the beginning, Joe made it clear that he
was no theologian. "I don't know what epistemology
is, I have never met an anarthrous predicate nomina-
tive, and I use my one-volume systematic theology as
a doorstop. I can't do all that intellectual argumenta-
tion you guys do, but I want to help people know the
real Jesus."[18]

God has a wonderful way of using people who love him
and seek to understand his Word. Joe did not have a
graduate degree, he never went to seminary, and he wasn't
ordained. But he loved God, knew what the Bible said, and
cared about truth. His Bible knowledge and association with
informed and compassionate fellow believers kept him from
being carried away by all kinds of strange teachings. Quickly
he learned how to help others separate error from truth.
    Joe is a difference maker who is not swayed by false
teachings. We must be careful to do the same.

Chapter Highlights

‡ Difference makers learn from those who are leaders.
  Look for difference makers who are good models.
  Determine to be a difference maker who can be an
  example to others.
‡ We don't have many good models today. In part, this
  is because many people's lives are out of balance.
  There is strength in balance.
‡ To keep our lives in balance and to maintain account-
  ability, each of us needs a personal board of directors.
‡ Effective difference makers select their teachers care-
  fully and learn from them. Be aware of strange
  teachings and carefully evaluate what your teachers
  say.
‡ To evaluate teachers find out about their credentials.
  Look at whom the teachers quote and how the quotes

are used. Be alert for unbalanced teaching that emphasizes some parts of Scripture but overlooks the rest. Be wary of sweeping statements. Watch how the teacher responds to criticisms and look at his or her students. Get help from teachers and writers whom you trust. Be a consistent Bible student.

13

Surprised by Prayer

Almost ten years ago our telephone rang one Saturday morning and the caller passed on the message that I would not have to teach my Bible class the next day. Sometime during the preceding night, an intruder had entered our church building and set it on fire. The sanctuary had been destroyed and all the members were to meet Sunday in the gymnasium of a nearby high school.

A few weeks after the fire, when the congregation was still considering their plans to rebuild, I was asked to present a series of talks on prayer. I resisted the suggestion because nobody is qualified to act as an expert on prayer. After some gentle persuasion, however, I accepted the challenge. And the person who learned the most about prayer was me.

Principle Number 14:
Commit Yourself to Prayer

It is easier to write about prayer than to pray; easier to study books on prayer, read sermons about prayer, and look up Bible verses about prayer than to take the time to approach God in prayer. Yet the writer of Hebrews asked for prayer and wrote: "I particularly urge you to pray."[1]

In preparing for my talks, I learned what I could from others, spent a lot of time in prayer myself, and made some refreshing discoveries.

Prayer is work. I was surprised several years ago when I came across a book titled *The Struggle of Prayer.* I had always had difficulty finding time to pray and keeping my mind from wandering, but nobody had ever suggested that prayer might be a struggle for all of us.[2]

John Knox defined prayer as "an earnest and familiar talking with God." It takes time from our busy schedules. It demands that we become still, even though our society views stillness as a waste of time. Prayer seems like an unnatural activity, an embarrassing interruption to our lives in the fast lane.[3] The Devil is likely to be active in resisting our efforts to pray because prayer undermines his schemes. Often we find our prayer times interrupted by ringing telephones, distracting surroundings, and wandering minds. Is it so surprising that prayer is a struggle?

There are a few techniques (gimmicks might be a more accurate word) that I rely on to help me in the struggle of prayer.

I schedule a regular time every day to pray. For me this is early in the morning before the phone starts ringing and interruptions begin. I try to pray in the same location, at least when I am at home. I like to write a prayer almost every day because writing focuses my attention and keeps my mind from wandering. Often I refer to a little notebook where I keep prayer requests. Part of the notebook lists the people and topics that I try to pray about daily. Another section is divided into seven segments where I record particular concerns and specific individuals whom I bring before God on different days of the week. I also keep a list of specific prayer requests and make a note when God answers.

What works for me may not be best for you. The main thing is to find some structure that will hold you accountable and help you deal with the work that is characteristic of prayer.

Prayer starts with God. I resisted this idea when I first encountered it.[4] I had always been inclined to barge into

God's presence and tell him what I needed. It was liberating to realize that God might want to communicate with me. I now realize that a time of prayer can start by asking God to guide my thinking and the content of my prayers.

This means that prayer should involve quiet adoration and praise, which focuses my mind on what God is like. It also means that prayer can be guided by Scripture. Reading a psalm, for example, can point our minds to a number of God's attributes. Often I jot these down. Prayer must also involve a personal yielding to God's sovereign will and direction. It is easy to tell God what we want or need, but he is more interested in guiding us to what we should have.

Because prayer starts with God, it involves listening. Sometimes when I start praying or writing a prayer I will say, "Lord put in my mind what you want me to write and to pray about." He often seems to implant ideas into my mind, and my prayer time goes in directions that I had not intended or expected. As I grow in my understanding I hope to become less inclined to say "Give me," and more inclined to say "Change me."

Prayer is learned. The disciples asked Jesus to teach them how to pray. Apparently they saw something in the Lord's life that they wanted and needed, so they asked for a way to duplicate his intimacy with the Father.

We can learn by reading about prayer, by hearing others talk about it, by looking at Bible passages that describe it. Our learning, however, must include the experience of praying. We learn by doing.

Prayer is tied to action. Prayer is not something that occupies an out-of-the-way corner of life. It deals in the realities of daily living. In the life of Jesus, daily activities and daily prayers went together. Before he made a decision or attempted any ministry, Jesus set aside time for rest and prayer. After praying he got involved in effective action:

preaching, teaching, healing, meeting the needs of people. "To pray about it and leave it to God can be an unbiblical cop-out," according to Rowland Croucher. "Prayer is not an alternative to battle action: it accompanies battle action." In the life of Jesus, prayer and action remained in healthy balance.[5]

Once we see the importance of prayer, we are more likely to pray at a specific time each day. That discipline will often encourage other spontaneous short prayers as we go about our day. Prayer becomes an ongoing communication between a Christian and the Creator.

For the Christian difference maker, prayer is crucial. When we are guided by the sovereign God, our efforts will be Christ honoring and long lasting.

At times the only thing we can do to make a difference is to pray. Sometimes that is also the most effective thing we can do.

Pulling It All Together

The people of God in the Old Testament had an elaborate system of rituals and sacrifices to atone for their sins and bring themselves into favor with God. When Jesus Christ, God's Son, came to earth, the need for such sacrifices ended. Christ "died for sins, once for all, the righteous for the unrighteous," to bring us to God. Most of the book of Hebrews deals with this subject. Christ, we read "appeared once for all at the end of the ages to do away with sin by the sacrifice of himself."[6] Christians believe that because of Christ's sacrifice we can have forgiveness of sins and life everlasting. No longer do we have to rely on the elaborate sacrificial offerings that were so central to Jewish religious life.

Today God asks for a different sacrifice from us. This sacrifice is not to pay for our sins. Christ has already done that. Instead, God wants us to present our bodies and our minds to him as "living sacrifices" so we can do God's "good, pleasing and perfect will."[7]

Near the end of the book of Hebrews there is a sobering statement about sacrifices. It summarizes all that has been said in these chapters: "Through Jesus, therefore, let us continually offer to God a sacrifice of praise—the fruit of lips that confess his name. And do not forget to do good and to share with others, for with such sacrifices God is pleased."

If you want to be a difference maker whose activities are pleasing to God, get into the habit of praising him and doing good to others.[8] When our lives focus on pleasing ourselves or pleasing others, we will ultimately feel empty and unfulfilled. If we determine to live lives that are pleasing to God, we will find inner peace, a deep sense of joy, and true fulfillment. God pleasers are the best kind of difference makers.

Gilbert Bilezikian wants to be a God pleaser. He freely admits that (like all of us) he has fallen short of his goal, but there are few people whom I admire as much as this man whom almost everybody calls Dr. B.

Perhaps you have never heard of this quiet, sensitive gentleman with the French accent. His colleagues at the college where he teaches know him as a scholar whose books and articles are carefully researched, influential, and sometimes controversial. His academic work is significant, but his influence in the lives of his students has been even greater.

Many years ago Dr. B had a class of young collegians who were taking his biblical studies course as a requirement for graduation. The professor taught his subject matter well, while gently raising issues that unsettled some class members. "What are you going to do with your one and only life that will last forever?" he would ask.

One student was sure he knew the answer to that

question. He was going to get his degree as quickly as possible and return to a lucrative family business in Michigan. But Dr. B's classes challenged that comfortable plan and the student made the difficult decision to change his career direction.

With the help of the professor and a few other visionary students, the young man led a little group that founded a church. It was designed to reach the secular, unchurched suburban population in a residential area north of Chicago. The new congregation began meeting in a movie theater and their numbers grew rapidly. Today, Willow Creek Community Church is one of the largest and most effective congregations in America. It has reached thousands of unchurched people and won them to Christ. Its unusual, refreshing, but solidly biblical approach to disciple making has attracted attention from around the world. Its widely respected senior pastor, Bill Hybels, is the former student who was challenged and has been encouraged consistently by his former professor, Gilbert Bilezikian.

Dr. B may not fully realize this, but his example has inspired many people. It has inspired his family. It has inspired hundreds of professional colleagues and students. It has inspired many of the people at Willow Creek Community Church. It has inspired me. Because of his impact I have become more devoted to challenging *my* students to think seriously about what they plan to do with their lives that will last forever. By his example, his words, and his consistent determination to please Christ, Gilbert Bilezikian has been a difference maker.

To Recap

In the past ten chapters, we have discussed fourteen principles from Hebrews that mark the lives of people who make a difference. They are summarized in the following chart.

How to Be a Difference Maker

---

1. Get and keep the right mindset (Hebrews 12:1).

2. Keep working to clear out the sin in your life (Hebrews 12:1).

3. Set some goals and stick with them (Hebrews 12:1).

4. Fix your eyes on Jesus (Hebrews 12:2).

5. Expect resistance (Hebrews 12:3, 7, 12).

6. Build relationships (Hebrews 12:14).

7. Keep a long range perspective (Hebrews 12:16, 17).

8. Be a people helper (Hebrews 13:1, 3).

9. Show hospitality (Hebrews 13:2).

10. Be a marriage builder (Hebrews 13:4).

11. Be content with what you have (Hebrews 13:5).

12. Learn from those who are leaders (Hebrews 13:1, 17).

13. Select your teachers carefully (Hebrews 13:9).

14. Commit yourself to prayer (Hebrews 13:18, 19).

Part Three
Difference Making in Daily Life

Family Difference Makers

*C*arrie B. Ponder *got an award recently.*

She hadn't expected others to notice what she did. But her picture and a feature story about her achievements appeared on the front page of a big-city newspaper.

"Raising a child alone is difficult enough," said the man who presented Mrs. Ponder with her Adult Achievement Award. "Bringing up eight children is even more difficult. Doing it in the inner city with no child support is seemingly impossible. But Carrie Ponder did it, and for that reason, we salute her today."

Over fifteen years ago, when Mrs. Ponder's husband left, her youngest daughter was barely out of diapers and the oldest son, Rhinold, was still in his teens. The young mother knew that life would not be easy but she had learned a basic lesson from her grandparents in Mississippi: Be self-reliant and try to find resources in the community. She was able to get a series of low-paying jobs, often at the schools where her children were enrolled. She used food stamps to buy provisions for the family table and she looked for opportunities to feed her children's minds. Every weekend, Mrs. Ponder scanned the newspapers for news about reduced or free tickets to plays, museums, and even the opera.

"When there was very little money, I would just pack a lunch, go to a park, and sit around the Art Institute," Carrie told a reporter. "Sometimes we would ride on a bus from one end of the city to the other and talk about architecture." At home, the family would watch the 10 p.m. news on television and sit at the breakfast table next morning discussing world events—far beyond their poor and destitute neighborhood.

Once the family had to move from their three bedroom apartment because the elderly landlords were selling the building. It wasn't easy to find accommodations for a family with eight children, but eventually they found a "last resort" apartment in the worst neighborhood that any of them had seen. One week later the building burned down and the family lost everything. But they all were alive and still healthy so they tried to forget about their lost possessions. With the help of the Red Cross and friends they found another apartment where the mother still lives.

None of this determined lady's children has dropped out of school or turned to drugs and crime. Her sons and daughters, now ranging in age from nineteen to thirty-one, are college students or graduates of prestigious institutions such as Princeton, Northwestern, and the Universities of Chicago and Pennsylvania. The oldest child is a lawyer, the youngest is a dancer with the Alvin Ailey American Dance Theater in New York City.

"Though poor of pocket, we were not poor of mind and spirit," said one of the sons following the award ceremony. "Our mother set the leadership example."

"You can have a lot of money," said another, "but my mother has produced and reared eight children who are productive members of society. To me there is no richer person in the world."

I wish I had been there to applaud when they presented the award.[1]

Through persistence and a determination to succeed, Carrie Ponder helped her kids beat the odds of giving in to the limitations of poverty. She has been a difference maker where it matters most—in her own family.

Drugs and Domestic Difficulties

While they were growing up in the inner city, the Ponder children saw many individuals and families whose lives were ruined by addiction. Substance abuse has long been common in the inner city and is increasingly present in the suburbs as well. Drug and alcohol problems are so prevalent that employers and government agencies have developed expensive testing and rehabilitation programs.

Recently, however, research in business and industry has suggested that addictive behavior—alcohol and chemical dependency—is now the number one work-place problem.[2] Productivity and concentration at work are more likely to be influenced by conflicts in the home. Wherever they live or work, employees are affected by the stress that comes from troubled marriages, divorces, financial worries, or problems with children. Domestic difficulties can even lead to chemical dependency. There are exceptions, of course, but normally a person with a supportive family and a stable home life is less likely to develop addictions.

I am amazed at the number of professional journal articles, popular books, and seminars that focus on family life. Church retreats, marriage enrichment weekends, and dozens of call-in talk shows try to address our difficulties at home. The topics covered are diverse: physical abuse, divorce, unfaithfulness, incest, communication breakdowns, AIDS, money, step families, older relatives, school problems, dysfunctional homes. These and a host of other issues continually disrupt family life.

Sometimes, it seems that no one can escape. Can anyone grow up in a family without being wounded? At times most of us feel like failures in our family relationships. We go to weddings and wonder if these new marriages will survive. We bring children into the world and hope that they will "turn out okay," even though all sensitive parents harbor insecurities about the future of their sons and daughters.

We aren't surprised that marriage counselors and family therapists exist in great numbers because we know how hard it is to build solid marriages and good families in a world that constantly tears at those relationships.

In spite of all this, sometimes God surprises us and uses us to be difference makers at home.

I thought of this recently when I heard a lady named Nancy Beach tell a church congregation about her father. While he may never have won any awards for his parenting activities, that father made a profound difference in the life of his daughter.

"He gave me time," the young woman said in her tribute.

"He provided a sense of security while I was growing up." He taught his family clear values: unambiguous views of right and wrong. Over the years he became a model of the kind of husband Nancy Beach would eventually find and marry. By the way he lived—and continues to live—this father gave his family a glimpse of what the heavenly Father is like.

Some people never had fathers like that. Others feel that they could never be fathers or mothers who could make such a positive impact on their families.

But the creative passion of Carrie Ponder and the quiet influence of Nancy Beach's father show that we can overcome obstacles and make a difference at home. It is never too early or too late to start.

Family Difference Making Is a Challenge

Near the beginning of the Bible we are introduced to a man named Abraham and his wife, Sarah. Several times God promised Abraham that he would be the father of a great nation. His offspring would become as numerous as the stars in the sky or the grains of sand on the beach. In all of history, perhaps no other person has been given such potential for being a difference maker in his family.

But things didn't go smoothly for Abraham and Sarah. They encountered a number of obstacles, including some family problems similar to those that many of us face today.

To start, God promised large numbers of descendants but Abraham and Sarah had no children. Apparently they had an *infertility* problem in an era when childlessness was seen as an expression of God's displeasure. It is hard to make a difference at home if you want children but can't get pregnant.

To some around him it might have appeared that Abraham had a problem with *lack of direction* in his life. God told him to gather up all his possessions, animals, and servants and make a major move. When Abraham obeyed and set out on his long journey, he didn't have the remotest idea where he was going. He went by faith expecting that God would lead. Today we admire Abraham's courage, but sometimes we are critical of other people of faith who trust the same God. We label them as irresponsible when they flounder with no apparent goals or direction but continue trying to discover the paths that God has for them.

Did some of his neighbors think that Abraham had the problem of *instability?* He lived in a foreign land, residing in tents instead of in a house with a foundation. We know that roots are important if families are to feel secure and stable. But in our complex society it can be difficult to find stability. Decent housing is hard to locate at an affordable price. At times it isn't possible to stay at the same job or in the same neighborhood for a long period of time.

In Egypt Abraham had a *dishonesty* problem. Sarah was so beautiful that her husband was afraid she might be stolen and he might be killed by some jealous suitor. So Abraham pretended that Sarah was his sister. This deceit was nearly disastrous. In modern times dishonesty can be equally devastating, especially when we practice it in front of our families.

The Bible never states this directly, but Abraham and Sarah also might have had a problem with *impatience*. This is understandable. When they reached advanced years, they still had no children. Sarah's solution was for her servant girl Hagar to have sex with Abraham and bear the children that would fulfill God's promise. When Hagar got pregnant, however, Sarah became angry and later drove the young mother and her son into the wilderness. All was not quiet in the family of Abraham! Many people today can understand both the problem of impatience and the family tensions that result from it.

Abraham was one hundred years old and Sarah was in her nineties when Isaac, the long-promised son, finally was born. Raising a young boy when they were senior citizens must have been a challenge for both the parents and the son. Being a parent at any age can be difficult.

Throughout all of this, however, Abraham learned some valuable lessons. These lessons are helpful to any of us who want to be difference makers in our families. *Abraham learned the importance of obeying God.* Even though he didn't know where he was going, Abraham packed his possessions and moved because God had told him to go.[3]

Abraham learned to provide for his family, without griping, even when it was inconvenient and to his own disadvantage. When Abraham and his nephew Lot decided to part company, the older man let the younger choose where he would live. Lot selected the most fertile land and left the rest to his uncle. Sometime later, Lot was captured and all of his possessions were stolen, but Uncle Abraham came to the rescue. Lot was brought back to his relatives and the lost possessions were recovered.[4]

Abraham learned that we fail when we try to manipulate circumstances. It was Sarah's idea to have Abraham father a child through Hagar, but Abraham appeared to give no resistance. This was not what God intended, and a great deal of pain and misery grew out of this "ill-conceived" plan.[5]

Most important, perhaps, *Abraham learned that God could be trusted.* Even though Sarah was barren and very old, she bore a child. Through this experience Abraham discovered that nothing is too hard for the Lord—even having an elderly woman give birth. Later when God told him to sacrifice his long-awaited son, Isaac, Abraham did not resist. The old man had learned that God was in control and would provide for Isaac's safety. When his son was old enough to get married, Abraham assumed that God would provide the right woman at the right time. A servant was sent to find a wife, and no hint was made that the mission might not be successful. When he died Abraham had seen little evidence that God would raise up a great nation from Isaac's descendants, but a lifetime had shown that God would do as he promised.[6]

It is difficult for any of us to hold on to ideas like these when things are not going as we had expected and when God seems far away. As we have seen in earlier chapters, God doesn't promise to keep us from trials or to deliver us immediately when the going gets tough. But he does promise to stick with us,[7] and he can be trusted. What we see as a disaster, God can use for good.

I saw this several years ago in the life of a childless couple whose faith and dependence on God made a permanent impact on many lives, including my own.

David Smith was a seminary student who met every week with a little group that used to share together and pray in my office. He was one of the finest students that I ever had. Everybody who met him, liked him—that's still true. He was friendly, outgoing, handsome, concerned about people, seemingly self-assured, and deeply committed to serving Christ. His wife, Nancy, was quieter but equally competent, dedicated, and likable.

One spring, Dave told our little group that he and Nancy would soon have their first child. Everybody was delighted until the young parents discovered that their baby was developing normally in every way except one: It would be born without a brain and a skull.

The doctors agreed in their recommendation: terminate the pregnancy. For the Smiths, who had always opposed abortion, that was not an option.

Instead, they decided to pray. They started by asking for guidance about how to pray and concluded that they should pray for healing. After taking their problem to the top physicians in their area, they went to the Great Physician. Then they asked their friends to pray for healing with them.

I don't suppose I was the only one who struggled with this request. My wife and I had developed a real love for this young couple. None of us doubted that the God who worked so wonderfully in the life of Abraham could work in the body of that tiny unborn baby. But were the parents being unrealistic when they asked their friends to "pray that God will produce a normal and healthy and complete child; one that will be able to walk and talk and clap and sing and think and reason and hear and see, just as any other child"?

We talked about this in our little Wednesday morning group. Dave and Nancy were well aware that God might not heal. Their faith and confidence in God was not dependent on a miracle. They believed that God could be trusted, that his will would be done, and that he would be honored no matter what the outcome.

But the Smiths also believed that their position as parents required them to ask God for his miraculous intervention.

The doctor who was caring for the young couple backed out of the case. In her mind the baby was already dead.

Other doctors did not want to get involved and the couple had no medical support until they found a physician who was willing to stick with them through the pregnancy.

The baby was carried full term—kicking and moving inside the mother like babies do in the weeks prior to birth. After a long and difficult labor, a baby girl was born—finely featured, smooth skinned.

Each parent held her briefly and cried. But Bethany Joy Smith had died because she didn't have a brain.

In the weeks that followed, Dave and Nancy Smith grieved. There were many tears and a deep sadness.

But there were no regrets about their child who had lived in the womb, spent such a brief time with her earthly parents, and gone to be with her heavenly Father. Like several hundred others, my wife and I watched a young couple show their belief that God knew best, during and after an incredibly difficult time in life. God didn't choose to heal their baby, but through this painful experience he strengthened all of us personally and spiritually.

In the midst of their ordeal, I invited Dave and Nancy to speak to a group of about two hundred somewhat complacent church members, many of whom had been Christians for a number of years. The Smiths came before the birth of their baby and again, several months after the baby's death. Never before or since have I seen that group of believers so touched and so challenged by a simple example of modern faith and confidence in God.

Dave and Nancy Smith were young parents who had been used by God to be difference makers in many of our lives. Now, perhaps, their example has influenced you.

Family Difference Making Takes Effort

Not long ago, a young author from Australia made the rounds of North American bookstores, autographing copies of his book on how to be happy. When someone asked the secret of happiness, the Australian smiled—which is what we might expect from a man who is a self-proclaimed expert on happiness and whose book was selling well.

"To be honest," he said, "I don't say anything really new or different in this book." If you want to be happy, according to the smiling Australian, you should decide to be happy, think positively, surround yourself with happy people, think healthy thoughts, set goals, and take risks. Many others have said the same thing, but the happy author claimed that he "just packaged the thoughts so they become useful."

Most of us have read books—including books on the family—that say little or nothing new. But the ideas may be packaged in new ways so they become more useful. Even if the concepts are old, the authors remind us of things that we easily forget.

I don't think there are any new and creative formulas for being a difference maker in the family, but some old principles need to be dusted off periodically and reapplied.

Get into the habit of showing respect. Family difference makers show respect for one another. According to my dictionary respect involves treating others with consideration and courtesy, holding others in high regard, expressing appreciation.

The Bible tells wives to respect their husbands, husbands to respect their wives, children and parents to respect each other, and Christians to show respect to everyone, including non-believers.[8] The best counselors show respect for the people who are counseled, even when these people make big mistakes or do things that are sinful and foolish. We don't condone or respect the behavior, but we show consistent courtesy and regard for people who have been created in the image of God.

We all make unwise decisions, but sometimes we look back and see things that we don't regret. My wife and I always tried to respect our kids, even when we disagreed with some of their decisions or actions and even when we felt the need to give discipline. We have always tried to avoid put-downs, sarcastic comments, biting humor, or unkind verbal jabs. We have prayed consistently for our children (we still do), have asked God for wisdom, and have tried to be consistently loving. In so doing we have been better able to make a difference in the lives of our two daughters.

You may be at odds with some family member, but try to remind yourself of what is good in that person and worthy of respect. Then look for opportunities to say the positive things that you have been thinking. In a book about raising "positive kids in a negative world," Zig Ziglar identified kindness and respect as the two most important parental characteristics.

Keep aware of your own attitudes. A local businessman recently posted a big sign in front of his store: "FOR SALE. ONE SET OF ENCYCLOPEDIAS—NEVER USED. TEENAGE SON KNOWS EVERYTHING."

A few days after the sign went up, a passing motorist dropped $150 cash on the counter and toted away twenty-five never-opened volumes of the Encyclopedia Britannica.

The sign was a good gimmick and clearly it worked to sell the books. But it probably didn't do much to build good rapport between that father and his teenager. Had I been the son, I would have viewed that sign as a not-too-subtle put-down.

Sometimes we fail to make a difference at home because our attitudes and our actions create division. Jesus told his followers to take a look at themselves before finding fault in others.[9]

You won't make much of a positive difference in your family if you tend to be rigid, hypercritical, unwilling to forgive, prejudiced, stubborn, overcommitted, unwilling to address difficult issues, engrossed in a workaholic lifestyle, addicted to television, quick to get angry, likely to lose your temper, never willing to admit that you might be wrong, or inclined to show a holier-than-thou attitude. If you sometimes find your attitudes and actions resembling parts of this list, like I do, ask God and your family members to help you change.

But be prepared for a surprise. Many of us are blind to weaknesses that our family members see very well. If you express a willingness to change, your kids or your spouse might be brave enough to tell where you *really* need change.

Don't lose sight of the other person's perspective. When our daughters were teenagers, two issues bothered me: their choice of fashions and their choice of boyfriends. At times both seemed to be a little weird!

One afternoon I was driving our older daughter to work and I asked—gently and in a way that I tried to make non-threatening—about her spiked hair, black lipstick, and baggy, loose-fitting clothes.

"Don't worry about it Dad," she said in a refreshing display of teenage honesty and insight. "People don't dress like this in their twenties. I'm just going through a stage."

The stage lasted longer than her mother and I would have liked, but all three of us worked to maintain good communication with each other. We tried to avoid over-reacting, defensiveness, and manipulative behavior. When we disagreed, we tried to see things from the other person's perspective.

Express yourself lovingly and honestly. How can we hope to be difference makers if we never communicate? Every marriage counseling book in my library says something about communication breakdowns. When there are problems in relationships there often are problems with communication.

The essence of good communication is to express

yourself honestly and with an attitude of respect. The New Testament talks about speaking the truth in a loving manner,[10] but communication involves more than words. We communicate by our gestures, facial expressions, tone of voice, acts of kindness, even our lifestyles. Sometimes we convey a message most effectively by saying nothing but by living lives that have an impact.[11] We have all heard that actions speak louder than words. Sometimes actions also can be a powerful way to make a difference.

Ted Engstrom may have had this in mind when he described the influence of his father. "From my dad, years ago, I learned what God could do through a man, even with little education, committed to serving Him. He mentored me, not so much with words of counsel but rather with his committed, exemplary life as husband, father, mechanic, and lay preacher. He never 'unsaid' with his life what he said with his lips."[12]

Try to avoid communication roadblocks. We slip into these behaviors and ways of speaking without thinking, especially when we are frustrated. They not only stifle communication, but they also prevent us from being effective difference makers.

Some of the roadblocks are easily spotted: nagging, name-calling, use of loaded words (like "you always. . ." or "you never. . ."), giving lectures, or making vague insinuations. Sometimes we stifle communication by making exaggerated comments such as "You are the dumbest person in the whole school" or "If I've told you once, I've told you a billion times: don't exaggerate."

Double messages also get us into trouble. Often they involve saying one thing and doing something different. When a father tells one of his children, "I love spending time with you" and then is always too busy to get together, the child gets a confusing double message. Here again, the actions usually carry more weight than the words.

Hypocrisy is a special kind of double message that slips into the lives of Christians when what we do doesn't square with what we say. Almost the entire New Testament book of James deals with this issue. According to the writer, you can say all you want about what you believe, but your words don't mean anything unless they are backed up by actions. Abraham, who was called "God's friend," had faith and actions that worked together.[13]

Maybe this is at the core of making a difference in our families. We humbly submit to God and ask for his guidance. We are honest in saying what we believe, think, and feel, but then we back all of this up with the way we act.

Touching those who are closest. Some time ago, I heard about a visionary young man who grew up in the blue-collar neighborhood of a large English city. His own family life wasn't very good, but neither were the working conditions and living standards of his neighbors.

After graduating from the university, the young man was determined to change the British social system, to liberate the frustrated workers, and to bring improvement into the lives of the working class. His friends admired such determination, compassion, and lofty goals. They understood, too, when the student's best efforts were met with resistance and frustration.

One day he was discussing his unmet goals with a friend who made an astute comment. "You can't change the world," she said. "You can only touch the people near you."

That is good advice for any of us who want to be difference makers. Occasionally somebody like a Gorbachev may change the world or a part of it, but most of us can only touch the people nearby. That starts at home and sometimes at church.

Making a Difference in Your Church Family

Early in my teaching career, I resigned from my job at a midwestern Christian college and accepted a position at a struggling theological school in Philadelphia. We had a small faculty and a student body comprised largely of inner-city pastors who were overworked and underpaid but eager to learn.

The faculty didn't have individual offices. We all shared the same room and most of us had desks that were pushed up against each other. My desk was face to face with that of a young theologian who was largely unknown but full of potential and solid theological knowledge. Often he and I would converse with each other across our two desks and during that year together we became good friends. When the school where we worked merged with another institution, my colleague and I moved to different parts of the country and since that time we have only seen each other once or twice.

Even in those early days the young theologian had a passion to know God and to teach. He went on to establish a study center for pastors and seminarians, began producing a series of audio and video tapes, and has since written a number of in-depth, highly regarded books about the nature of God and Christian living. His ministry has made a difference in a lot of lives, including mine. I'm probably the only one who still calls him Bob. Everyone else knows him as a scholar, theologian, and sensitive teacher named R. C. Sproul.

R.C. has devoted his professional career to careful study of the Scriptures. He has written that Bible study involves careful, diligent, difficult work, and he has devoted himself to understanding and presenting the Scriptures in ways that will glorify God and strengthen the church.

Most of us are not theologians or Bible students who can read the texts in their original languages, give interesting lectures, and write carefully reasoned theological books. But most of us *are* involved in churches. We teach Sunday school classes, sing in choirs, care for little children, take teenagers on overnight camping trips, prepare church suppers, and serve on committees.

In some churches these activities, all needed and useful, distract believers from the goals of worship, spiritual growth, and evangelism. Church politics, church squabbles, and church socials sometimes pull congregations in the direction of making the church little more than a neighborhood social club. Congregations like these may be busy places, but they tend to be spiritually lethargic.

In contrast spiritually alive churches are filled with individuals who are making a difference because the people want to know God better and have a genuine servant mentality. In a church near our home, for example, nobody is accepted as a member unless he or she has attended regularly for at least a year, demonstrated an understanding of basic Christian doctrine, met with the church leaders, and found a place of service within the local congregation. When they are introduced as new members, their names are read along with their place of service.

Energized for service. Do you remember the story of the mother who came to Jesus and asked if her sons, both of whom were disciples, could be seated in a place of prominence—one on either side of the Lord—when he established his kingdom? When the other disciples heard about this request they became indignant and Jesus had to intervene in their squabble.[14]

In this world, he said, the greatest people are those who have power, position, and authority. In the Christian life, however, the greatest people are servants.

This was a revolutionary statement that Christians are reluctant to accept even today. In the society where we live, greatness is measured by the number of people we manage, the amount of money we possess, the influence we have in our careers and professions, the numbers of books we have written, or the attention we attract. But God considers all of this to be irrelevant. He measures greatness by the commitment and attitudes we show, the people we help, the unseen things we do for others, the humility we genuinely desire, the gifts that we give, the willing service that is part of our way of life.

Thirty or forty years ago, every poll of outstanding leaders included the name of Albert Schweitzer. Theologian, scientist, philosopher, physician, university professor, humanitarian, musician—he was all of these and more. Before the age of thirty he had earned an international reputation as a scholar and an organist known for his ability to perform the works of Bach. Even those who disagreed with his theology recognized his brilliance and his true greatness. In 1952 he was awarded the Nobel Peace Prize.

But Albert Schweitzer left all of this and went to a place called Lambaréné in French Equatorial Africa. There, in a run-down chicken coop, he began to meet with impoverished Africans who came for medical treatment. Slowly this grew into a hospital and medical station. He used his $33,000 Nobel prize money to expand the hospital and to set up a leper colony.

Maybe the world itself knows that servanthood is the essence of greatness. We revere, admire, laud, and sometimes fear a person of power, but we genuinely love and respect the person who serves. Many people strive to be successful but we know, down deep, that true greatness is found in the one who gives. Even Jesus "did not come to be served, but to serve, and to give his life as a ransom for many."[15]

Difference makers at church. Few people are as brilliant or outstanding as Albert Schweitzer, but every one of us can be a servant difference maker in our own church. How do we do it?

First, make up your mind that it's worth doing. People who accept church positions in response to arm-twisting and coercion rarely make much of a difference because they aren't really self-motivated to serve. These are the people who resign at the first opportunity and leave the work to somebody else. Too often the "somebody else" is the over-burdened pastor.

Second, find and seek to develop your spiritual gifts. These, as we mentioned earlier, are special abilities and potential skills that come from the Holy Spirit and enable us to minister within the church in a way that benefits "the common good."[16] When people who want to serve end up disliking it, this is often because they are serving in the wrong capacity. People who serve in ways that use their spiritual gifts more often find fulfillment and delight in serving.

Periodically I get a call from someone at the church where we are members asking if I will be on a board or committee. My answer is always the same: no. This isn't because I am being uncooperative or disinterested, but I have learned that my gifts are not in administration. I can do it, but I hate it. There are other areas of service that fit my gifts, abilities, and temperament much better. These are where I serve willingly, enthusiastically, and effectively.

In recent years several people have written books or designed tests to help Christians find their spiritual gifts. If these are available, use them. If not, go to the method that Christians have used since the founding of the church. Take a careful look at yourself. Ponder what you really do best, what fits your interests and training and personality. Read Romans 12 and 1 Corinthians 12 for a better understanding of spiritual gifts. Ask mature Christians who know you well what they see as your special areas of giftedness. If you still aren't sure, try out a few areas of service and see where you fit best.

Third, never forget that we are all servants. Resist the tendency to push for positions of prominence and authority.

If you humble yourself and serve effectively where you are now, the Lord, in time, will lift you up,[17] Or he might leave you where you are. If you maintain the mindset of being a servant and let God know that you are willing to let him lead, you can expect that he will show you what to do.

Fourth, look for models and be a model for others. Try to find people in the local church whom you can admire and from whom you can learn. Then seek out others whom you can encourage, help, teach, and serve.

The apostle Paul instructed older men and women to work with those who are younger.[18] Few churches seem to emphasize this biblical plan, and it also appears to be rare in theological colleges and seminaries. Over the years I have met a number of people who would genuinely like this type of mentoring input from older, more mature believers—but the opportunities aren't often available. If you are willing to be that kind of a spiritual guide, ask God to work first in your life and then to lead you, in his timing, to somebody who can guide you spiritually and/or whom you can guide. This kind of one-on-one relationship makes a powerful difference in the lives of others.[19]

Many churches are filled with people who complain and find fault. Often it seems the loudest complainers are the people who are least active in trying to make a difference in and through their churches. People who serve willingly are both fulfilled and effective as difference makers.

One at a Time

Some difference makers influence hundreds or thousands of people, but that isn't true for most of us. Instead we start with our families or fellow church goers and influence a few people, often one at a time.

Recently I heard the story of a businessman who went with his wife for a few days of relaxation at an oceanfront hotel. One night a violent storm lashed the beach and sent massive breakers crashing against the shore.

Next morning, the businessman got up early and went for a walk to see what damage had been done during the night. As he strolled, he saw that the beach was covered with starfish that had washed ashore in the waves and now were several feet from the water. Once the morning sun broke through the dissipating clouds, the starfish would dry out and die.

Farther along, the strolling vacationer encountered a young boy who was picking up starfish, one at a time, and throwing them back into the water.

"Why are you doing that?" the man asked when he got closer to the boy. "Can't you see that one person will never make a difference in getting these starfish back into the water?"

"That's true," the boy said as he bent over, picked up another starfish, and tossed it into the ocean.

Then he smiled. "But I sure made a difference to that one!"

Chapter Highlights

Productivity and concentration at work are often influenced by emotional, marital, and family problems that come from the home. It is not easy to overcome family problems and to make a difference in the home.

Effective difference making often starts at home, especially if we remember some old principles:

‡ Get into the habit of showing respect to family members.
‡ Keep aware of your own attitudes towards family members, including attitudes that could create tension.

‡ Don't lose sight of the perspectives of other family members.

‡ Express yourself lovingly and honestly.

‡ Work at improving communication; avoid communication roadblocks.

‡ Make a difference by reaching out to those who are closest.

We can also make a difference in our own church families. To do so, make up your mind that difference making at church is worthwhile. Seek and develop your spiritual gifts. Never forget that we all are servants. Look for models and a be a model for others.

At home and at church, difference makers often influence one person at a time.

Community Difference Makers

Lizbeth Piedrasanta knows what it means to be down in the dumps.

A native of Guatemala City, Lizbeth finished college and went to an American graduate school where she earned a Master of Arts degree in counseling. From there she returned home to work in a counseling center that had been started by half a dozen young, creative, and sensitive Christian people helpers.

Counseling still is a new idea in Central America and believers who come for help with their problems often don't expect to pay; sometimes they are unable to pay. The small counseling center has always struggled financially, but despite these hardships it survives and continues to offer services in a location not far from the city dump.

In that dump, amidst the filth and garbage, hundreds of poverty stricken Guatemalans eke out an existence and raise their children, huddled together in make-shift huts that give minimal protection from the elements. I don't know how Lizbeth and her coworker Gladys first learned about the needs of those dump people, but one Christmas the two women decided to host a party. They were warned that their plan was dangerous. Strangers are not safe in the dump—especially two unprotected women.

But they persisted. Friends in Guatemala and the U.S. provided some funds. After weeks of negotiations, Lizbeth was able to make a purchase from a local blanket manufacturer who agreed to sell imperfect blankets for a reduced price. On the week before Christmas, the two determined women spent all of their waking hours making tacos for the children who had been invited to the party. Each would get a blanket for a gift and each would hear about Jesus, who loves all the little children—even those who live in a dump.

On December 24, the day when most Guatemalans celebrate Christmas, Lizbeth and Gladys lugged their blankets and their lovingly-prepared tacos to the party location.

Imagine their shock and disappointment when nobody was there. The two women were crushed. After all of their work, was the party being boycotted by distrustful parents? Were the people afraid to attend? Where were the children?

The answer was not long in coming.

For many of the dump people this was their first-ever Christmas celebration and everybody wanted to look nice for the occasion. The mothers had spent time washing clothes and bathing kids—a formidable task in the confines of a dump. The whole cleaning operation had taken longer than expected so the kids came late. But they came, wearing clean clothes and big smiles on their shiny, beaming faces.

The Christmas party was a huge success—so successful, in fact, that it has become an annual affair. It's much larger now and more people are involved in helping with the details and the tacos. College students and other caring Christians give up their own holiday celebrations at home and go to spend Christmas helping down in the dumps.

All of these people, inspired by the "dump-ladies" of Guatemala City, are making a difference in the community.

Neighborhood Difference Makers

When I was growing up, I used to hear a lot about far-away places with strange-sounding names. Missionaries would visit our church with artifacts and slides, urging us to give our lives to reach the heathen in darkest Africa or the lost and dying in China. I admired these people—I still do—but was it their intention to give us the idea that all of the excitement and action in this world occurs overseas?

In our church the young person who went into business or one of the professions was rarely challenged to serve the Lord or to make a difference at work. We got the impression that the real heroes of the faith were the missionaries. These dedicated people were closest to God, pastors were a few levels lower, and the rest of us made up the company of the less-committed at the bottom of the ladder.

Some of my high school friends went abroad as missionaries where they have had many years of effective service. They are making a difference. But others stayed at home to live in their neighborhoods and work in businesses, professions, universities, and factories. They too are making a difference.

Almost every day the newspapers carry stories about people who have made a difference in their communities or on the streets where they live. Most of us are surrounded by examples and opportunities.

‡ Valerie Bell, for example, is sometimes called the Kool Aid mom, because she tries to be available and willing to give a smile and a drink to the kids on her street who come home to empty houses. Despite the day-care centers and other facilities that provide for the kids of working mothers, many young people are lonely and by themselves after school. Valerie Bell is a committed Christian who is making a difference in the lives of these latchkey kids who live on her street and in her neighborhood. This isn't always convenient and neither is it easy, but a lot of us would agree with the Kool Aid mom that it's worth the effort.[1]

‡ Jethro Mann, the bicycle man of Belmont, North Carolina, repairs old bicycles and makes them available to anybody—child or adult—who wants to make a loan. Jethro, who retired in 1984, is active in his community, but

he remembers his childhood when there was no money for a luxury like a bicycle. Now the kindly man in Belmont loans them out, "ordinary bicycles for ordinary children." He believes that his unique hobby teaches kids to be responsible and shows that "if they'll take care of other people's things, they can't help but take care of their own." Jethro Mann really believes this works—and the kids all love him.

‡ Some of our neighbors recently moved to a community near a state prison. Through their church, these people have become involved as volunteers in the prison. They are making a spiritual difference in the lives of men and women behind bars and in the lives of prison families who struggle on the outside.

‡ I once had a student who frequently wrote little notes of thanks and encouragement. A thank-you note from a student is a rare thing; my former student sent them all the time—to teachers, friends, fellow church members, neighbors, and others. One year I decided to follow his example by writing one note of encouragement every week. My resolve wavered when I got busy with other things, but I enjoyed the surprised and warm reactions that came from some of the people who had received my cards.

‡ Meals-on-wheels is a church-run program in our community that provides hot meals for elderly and other housebound people. Volunteers take turns driving to the homes of grateful recipients, dropping off a meal and a little encouragement.

‡ In his insightful book on AIDS, Christian physician Gregg Albers writes about a lady named Alberta who met a young AIDS victim in the grocery store. They were surprised to discover that they lived in the same apartment complex and Alberta felt led to pray for her stricken neighbor. One morning she mustered the courage to bake a fresh blueberry pie and take it to his apartment. From this simple beginning, she built a friendship with a young man

who was dying and who had been forsaken by his friends and family. Alberta listened to his story, brought him hot meals, and told him about Christ.[2]

‡ When Chris Sommerfield died recently, he wasn't well known and I suspect he had a very small funeral. Over half a century ago, Chris and his young wife determined that they would spend their lives overseas as missionaries. They didn't need to be persuaded by emotional appeals or missionary slides; they felt called and they were ready to go.

But they couldn't go. Medical problems made this an impossible dream. The news was more than disappointing; the young couple was devastated.

But I still can picture old Mr. Sommerfield, many years later, reminding me about the Old Testament story of a battle between David and the Amalekites. There were six hundred in the army when the battle was about to begin, but two hundred were too exhausted to continue. So David left these physically weary people behind to stay with the supplies while the king and his four hundred warriors went to war and soundly defeated the enemy.

When they came back with the plunder, the four hundred warriors made it clear that the two hundred who remained behind should get nothing. "No my brothers," the king replied. "The share of the man who stayed behind with the supplies is to be the same as that of the man who went down to battle."[3]

Chris and Mildred Sommerfield hung on to that story. Their bodies were not strong enough to go into the front lines of missions, but they faithfully prayed, gave, continually wrote to missionaries all over the world, and kept their local church aware of the needs overseas. They sincerely believed that their service at home was as worthy and as needed as the work of those on the front lines of the mission fields abroad.

In a few years the Sommerfields may be forgotten to

almost all except God. But they were missionary difference makers, even though they never went far from their own neighborhood.

Do You Have a Passion?

Stories about people reaching out from their homes and into their neighborhoods or beyond can be inspiring and intimidating at the same time. You might be inspired by the example of others but intimidated because you have no idea how to do something similar.

Have you ever noticed that some of our greatest and most respected Christian leaders are driven by a specific passion? Often these people have a single purpose that guides most of their activities and keeps them going.

Dr. James Dobson, for example, has a passion for the family. In a statement of his organization's purpose, Dr. Dobson wrote "we have no other mission than to strengthen homes."

Billy Graham has a passion to preach the Gospel so men and women come to Christ. It is well known that he has resisted strong pressures to establish a university, go into politics, serve on government commissions, or do other worthwhile things that would distract him from his central purpose and passion.

There is need for multi-gifted people like Jim Dobson and Billy Graham, but what about ordinary people like you and me? Can we make a difference in our communities? How do we determine the purposes and passions of our own lives?

Maybe you could start by asking yourself a few questions. You may want to write down your answers and discuss these with one or two people who know you well. The first question might be the hardest:[4]

1. If you knew you could not fail, what would you do with your life?
2. What local, global, political, social, or church issues stir you emotionally? If you can't think of any, ask what issues *could* stir you up and get you excited.
3. What group of people do you feel most attracted to?
4. What area of need is of ultimate importance to you?
5. What area of your church's ministry would you most like to influence?
6. What do you love to do more than anything else?
7. What things do you do best?
8. How do you like to spend your free time?

Recently I gave this list to a group of men with whom I met on a regular basis. As we discussed our answers, we began to see where each of us had a special area of concern or passion. That is the area where each of us is most likely to make a difference. It is the area where we feel most fulfilled and able to develop our God-given abilities, talents, and interests.

Too Swamped to Make a Difference

In one of his books on effective leadership, Warren Bennis suggested two "laws" that probably fit us all—even if we aren't leaders.

First, routine work drives out all the fun and creative things you want to do. I wonder how many people want to go back to school, write a book, start a little business, get more involved at church, fix up the house, go to a special vacation spot, spend more time with the kids before they grow up—but never get around to doing what they say they want to do? It is fine to dream dreams, plan for the future, and think about our areas of passion, but often these get pushed aside by interruptions and more pressing things that have to be done. We want to make a difference but there isn't time to take meals to shut-ins, fix bicycles, visit prisons, teach Sunday school, take a class, sing in the church choir, disciple younger Christians, write letters to missionaries, serve on a committee, or do whatever else seems worthwhile.

The second Bennis law is similar to the first: Make whatever grand plans you will; you may be sure the unexpected or the trivial will disturb or disrupt them.[5]

If these laws apply to you, like they do to me, how can we prevent routine work, distractions, unexpected interruptions, or other hindrances from getting in the way and preventing us from pursuing our passions?

Part of the answer came to me many years ago when a visiting politician spoke on the campus of the Canadian university where I was an undergraduate. The visitor was a tall, gray-haired, stately woman who was making a difference in her party and in her country. When somebody asked how she got so much done, she replied that despite the interruptions and time stealers, most of us find the time to do what we *really* want to do.

Such an answer may ring hollow to an overburdened mother, a grown daughter who has to care constantly for an elderly parent, or a business person who has to stay on top of a host of details to keep the company solvent. These people feel that they have no time to pursue their areas of passion. Isn't it true, however, that with prior planning almost everybody can find at least a little time to edge toward their goals and do what they really want to do? If you feel overworked and overextended, maybe your first goal should be to determine how you can trim back your other activities and cut out some of the interruptions. You might need a friend or counselor to help as you think this through.

Every year in December, one man takes his appointment book for the new year and crosses off blocks of time for his creative activities, before the book gets filled with other things. Perhaps you could do something similar. Then you will be able to carve out at least a few opportunities to work toward your goals.

I have discovered that an inexpensive answering machine allows me to ignore the telephone so I have uninterrupted times to write. Like everyone else, I don't like those machines, but neither do I like having my thoughts interrupted by unexpected telephone calls. Now when the phone rings I ignore it until later.

Ultimately the goal is to pursue our areas of passion in ways that will make a difference for God, in our communities, and in our careers. The remainder of this chapter might help you reach that goal.

What Are Your Ambitions?

Not long ago I had lunch with a bright young man who apparently has no ambition. He faithfully attends church, is consistent in his personal prayer times, and does his job at a local bank, but he has no desire to stretch his mind through travel or reading, has no interest in further education, and doesn't care much about promotions at work. He thinks that some day he will get married and settle down "if the right girl comes along," but at present he isn't much motivated to find a wife.

My friend's lack of ambition was hard for me to handle. I know that some of his attitudes come from growing up in a home where nobody had much ambition or determination to make a difference. Maybe his lack of drive is partly a result of his laid-back personality. Even so, his attitude is very different from what I have seen for many years in my students and in myself. Many of us thrive on setting goals, making plans, being creative, completing degrees, getting ahead, developing potential, pursuing dreams, finding fulfillment, or thinking of ways to make a difference. In contrast my friend sits back and watches the world go by, unmoved by any ambitions or by desires to do something useful with his life.

The person with little or no ambition rarely becomes a difference maker. At the other extreme, people with too much ambition often aren't positive difference makers either.

Everybody knows that driving ambition can be a destructive force. People who are driven by personal ambition can be ruthless in their climb to the top. Some stop at nothing in order to get what they want; using and manipulating other people, hiding the truth, ignoring their families, flaunting their credentials, boasting about their accomplishments, or undercutting competitors. As they push to get ahead, their ambition destroys relationships, stifles creativity, and kills intellectual growth.

It is not surprising that the Bible warns against such selfish ambition. "Should you then seek great things for yourself?" Jeremiah asked his faithful secretary Baruch. The answer is immediate: "Seek them not."[6]

The apostle James is even more direct. "If you harbor bitter envy and selfish ambition in your hearts, do not boast about it. . . . Such 'wisdom' does not come down from heaven but is earthly, unspiritual, of the devil. For where you have envy and selfish ambition, there you find disorder and every evil practice."[7] Elsewhere in the New Testament selfish ambition is listed along with things like rage, jealousy, dissension, witchcraft, drunkenness, and orgies, all of which are part of our sinful nature. Some Christians in the Bible are criticized because they "preach Christ out of selfish ambition" and believers are instructed to "do nothing out of selfish ambition or vain conceit."[8] Clearly self-centered ambition is wrong.

But this does not mean that all ambition is wrong.

In describing himself, Paul said "it has always been my

ambition to preach the Gospel."[9] That was his passion and he pursued it ambitiously. In writing to the Thessalonians, he told the believers to "make it your ambition to lead a quiet life, to mind your own business and to work with your hands."[10] In referring to the quiet life, the apostle was not telling people to sit around, hands folded, doing nothing, without goals or aspirations. Instead, he appeared to be challenging them to work industriously, doing what each of them did best, steering away from gossip, and learning to be still before God.[11]

Ambitions are wrong if they are geared toward making us famous, powerful, rich, or even praised as difference makers. Ambition is sinful if it intends to hurt or embarrass others, create dissension, get revenge, prove how good you are, or "put down" people who are less successful or less ambitious.

In contrast, ambition can be a positive force when it helps us reach worthy goals. Such ambition is a significant power for good if it helps us please God,[12] serve and build up others, strengthen the church, live lives that are consistent with biblical teaching, develop our divinely-given talents, do God's will to the best of our abilities,[13] and make a positive difference in the world.

Are you ambitious? Ask yourself what you are ambitious about. Are your ambitious goals consistent with your abilities and gifts? Will your ambitions honor God? If your motives and goals seem right before the Lord, then go ahead and pursue your dreams. You may never be a prominent difference maker, but you will make an impact in the lives of others. And who knows? Perhaps God, who works through obedient and willing men and women, may use you to make a difference in ways that right now are beyond your wildest imagination.

Who Are Your Mentors?

Several years ago a team of researchers from Yale University published a book that attracted a lot of media attention. For several years the scientists studied young and middle-aged men, and the research raised interesting conclusions about getting established, building dreams, settling down, coping with middle life, and moving into old age.[14] One of the authors' key ideas concerned mentoring.

A mentor is a person who guides, inspires, encourages, advises, challenges, corrects, and serves as a model usually for somebody younger. Most often, the term *mentor* relates to one's work or career. An older physician or pastor, for example, serves as a mentor for some person who is younger and entering the same profession. Spiritual mentors are Christians who model godliness and encourage others in their walk with Christ.

According to Ted Engstrom in his book *The Fine Art of Mentoring*, the Christian mentor is more than a discipler. "Mentoring is a broader term describing the process of developing a man or a woman to his or her maximum potential in Jesus Christ in every [part of life]." A mentor is "a person who believes in the protégé and wants to see him or her win."[15] Mentors inspire their protégés, hold them accountable, challenge their thinking, push them to develop their fullest potential, and encourage them to be difference makers. "Above all," writes Engstrom, "a mentor seeks to instill in his [or her] charge the pursuit of excellence in service" for Christ.[16]

The Yale researchers concluded that the best mentors are eight to fifteen years older than the protégé—old enough for there to be an age difference between the two people but not old enough for the mentor to be a substitute parent. In practice, however, many good mentors are not eight to fifteen years older. On occasion, mentors are younger than their protégés and sometimes the two don't even know each other. It is possible for one person to admire, respect, appreciate, and learn from another, even though the two have never met.

It is also possible, and probably common, for each of us to have several mentors. Recently I tried to make a list of mine.

Jim Linden, for example, was a young professor at Purdue University who took me on as his first doctoral student. Later, he guided over fifty others through their doctoral programs and when he died, prematurely, I was invited to represent us all by bringing a eulogy at his funeral. Joseph Matarazzo, who later became president of the American Psychological Association, directed my internship program and taught me how to be a professional characterized by excellence. M. L. Custis, the physician who was mentioned in chapter 4, modeled what it was like to be a Christian professional. Junet Runbeck showed me how to teach in an undergraduate college.

Paul Tournier, the Swiss writer and counselor, had a writing style that did not impress me and I disagreed with some of his theology. Nevertheless, I was greatly influenced by his insights, his commitment to Christ, his gracious manner, and especially by his deep and genuine humility. He claimed to have a struggle with pride, but he was the most humble man whom I have ever met. Many years before meeting him (and writing a book about him), I had concluded that the essence of greatness is humility. In this respect, Tournier was the greatest man that I have ever known. He was a powerful mentor.

Unexpected mentoring. Mentors are not always successful people who model confidence or live in ways that others would want to follow. Sometimes tragedy, sickness, or even death has a powerful influence on the lives of others. Hard times in your life could make a significant difference in the lives of those who watch.

Near the end of his life, my own father admitted that he had not always been a good model and mentor. A few weeks before he died, however, I wrote a long letter of appreciation and reminded him of the famous actor who said that a play isn't over until the final act is done. In the fading months of his life, my father gave his most powerful example of mentoring. He taught me how to die with dignity. His last days were a radiant example of Paul's words to the Corinthians: "We do not lose heart. Though outwardly we are wasting away, yet inwardly we are being renewed day by day. For our light and momentary troubles are achieving for us an eternal glory that far outweighs them all. So we fix our eyes not on what is seen, but on what is unseen. For what is seen is temporary, but what is unseen is eternal."[17]

Mentors make a difference, sometimes without even knowing it. On the day that I started writing this chapter, I got a note from a former student whom I had not seen for at least five years. He was writing to express appreciation for the influence that my example had been in his life. I wasn't trying to be his mentor when he sat in my classes and visited in my home, but now I discover that he was watching me and learning from my example.

Who might be watching you? Your lifestyle, ways of doing your work, relationships with your family or business colleagues, manner of speech, responses to frustration, involvement with your local church—these might be making a difference in the life of some other person who is observing you.

Paul knew that people follow the example of other people. Often I have wondered how Paul was influenced, long before he became a Christian, when he stood and watched the martyrdom of Stephen.[18] Later Paul became a model for the believers in Philippi[19] and in one of his letters urged the believers to "Follow my example, as I follow the example of Christ."[20] The apostle was a mentor for younger men like Titus and Timothy, but he knew that many others were watching his example—just as they may be watching you.

This can be a sobering realization. By being an example and a mentor you can make a difference. If you aren't sure who should be your protégés, ask God to show you. Probably he will.

Then ask yourself, who are your mentors? Who are you watching right now, listening to, spending time with, emulating? Whose books are you reading (apart from this one)? It is true that if we have no mentors, we are less likely to grow. It is also true that we become like our mentors. So pick your heroes and mentors carefully, including those whom you admire from afar but never meet. In at least some ways you are likely to become like them.

For the Christian, Jesus Christ is the ultimate and only perfect mentor. The more we know him, the more we can be like him.

Paul Borthwick has written about a young corporate executive whose Christian character was seen and respected by his associates at work. One day the young man was asked how he was able to develop as a Christian leader in a highly competitive business environment. He answered in five words: "I chose a good mentor."

If you want to be a difference maker, choose good mentors and seek to be a good mentor.

Making a Difference at Work

Douglas LaBier is a psychiatrist who works with success-oriented young professionals who are troubled and emotionally damaged by their work and careers. Some are very successful. Many have made good progress in climbing the corporate ladder. They have earned significant promotions and enjoy big salaries, prestige, and lots of executive perks.

But they have come to the psychiatrist because their lives are empty, they are distressed by their own greed and ruthlessness, and they feel trapped by their careers and lifestyles. Many struggle to keep abreast of technical developments and changes in their fields. Most want a greater sense of fulfillment, but they don't want to be slaves to their companies and achievements. Many of these people have become workaholics, with neglected, angry families and a sense of inner turmoil and frustration. A few have reached the top and discovered that there isn't much there.[21]

Some of these outwardly successful people are making a difference, but they are hurting themselves and others in the process. Many have a passion and ambition, but are self-centered and insensitive to others. Some have followed mentors, but the mentors have not been good examples of healthy, balanced living.

These sad lives raise an important question. Can we be successful in our careers and effective in making a difference for good without falling into emotional turmoil like that of Dr. LaBier's patients? I believe the answer is yes.

In an interesting study of leadership, business writer Philip B. Crosby identified three areas that are necessary for effectiveness in the corporate and professional world. These three issues—building good relationships, striving for quality, and handling finances effectively—are called the foundation on which balanced, healthy lives and careers should be built. I would add two more: learning all you can and living in accordance with the biblical view of success. If we can build our careers, ministries, and families on these five foundations, then we can be successful, effective difference makers in our homes, in our communities, and beyond. And we can be difference makers who do not become emotionally crippled in the process.

1. *Build good relationships*. Billie Davis was a little girl in

the South during the Great Depression. Her family traveled between the cotton fields and fruit orchards looking for work and barely surviving in the process. One of her little brothers died of starvation and the family was always hungry.

A baker near one of the migrant worker camps felt sorry for the poor, starving people, so each day he would load a truck with day old bread and drive slowly through the dusty rows of shacks. A man in the back of the truck would throw bread to the ground as the truck passed by.

"I ran behind the truck with the rest of the people and got my bread," Billie Davis wrote many years later after she had become a college professor. "The bread had some nutrition, and I'm glad there were people compassionate enough to feed the poor. But how I hated that bakery! I despised the man who stood up there and threw me bread. I despised him because I had to trade my dignity, *myself*, for a loaf of bread."

One day Billie's family discovered a Sunday school and the little girl took her place, hesitantly, in a small red chair. The teacher did something that day that changed the young girl's life. The teacher didn't show pity, criticize, or preach against sin. Instead, she told the tiny girl that she was a child of God and that Jesus loved her.

Later, when Billie was eight years old, selling baskets on the street, a customer told her that she should be in school and that it was free. The girl couldn't believe it. Nothing that she knew about was free, so Billie walked to a public school and asked if what she had heard could be true. "They signed me up and gave me a desk," she wrote later, and they taught "that I could actually learn. I wasn't any different from the real people when I had the same opportunities and treatment."

As she grew up Billie Davis learned about Jesus, who showed compassion, accepted imperfect people, spent time with social outcasts, listened to those who were confused, criticized the spiritually proud, demonstrated mercy, and showed people how to find forgiveness for their sins.

"Poverty was not my worst problem," the woman wrote as she reflected on her childhood. "The main problem was not belonging—not belonging anywhere or with anyone." People need to belong. They need relationships. They need to be treated with respect and dignity.[22]

If you want to be a difference maker, learn to be sensitive to people. Treat them with kindness, courtesy, and dignity. You won't be a difference maker if you don't build relationships and if you aren't concerned about people.

2. *Strive for quality.* Several years ago two men decided to interview the top executives of America's best-run corporations. After Thomas Peters and Robert Waterman published *In Search of Excellence*, a book about their findings, there was a flurry of interest in quality. Articles, books, and seminars appeared with guidelines for building excellence into our businesses, careers, and lives.[23]

Some of that excitement has now passed, but the importance of excellence and quality has not. The best-run companies in the Peters-Waterman research group showed a deep respect for people, tried to keep things simple "despite overwhelming genuine pressure to complicate" matters, and never lost a commitment to building quality. Mediocrity was shunned, and so was the attitude that said "what we've done is good enough." Company growth tended to be less important than building quality. It was agreed that when quality comes first, growth follows automatically.

None of us can do everything well, but we all can do some things well. Decide what you want to do with quality—then make every effort to do it. "Striving for excellence in one's work, whatever it may be, is not only the

Christian's duty, but it is a basic form of Christian witness."[24]

3. *Handle finances effectively.* If success in this life depended on financial expertise, I probably would be a great failure. I barely understand the meaning of accounts receivable, cash flow, dividends, or net profit, and beyond that I am lost. When I try reading the prospectus of some investment or money market account, it looks to me like a legal statement or a computer manual—long strings of complicated words written in the worst possible English and meaning nothing, except maybe to the writer and a few experts.

But I recognize bills. (Like you, I have lots of experience with them.) I know how to balance a checkbook, I try to avoid credit cards, and I pay what I owe. It is not hard for any of us to see what happens when individuals, companies, churches, ministries, academic institutions, and governments commit money they don't have, to acquire things that they can't pay for later.

Sloppy, careless, irresponsible money management discredits any of us who control funds. Christian organizations become the brunt of jokes and are scorned if the money of donors is not managed with great care and integrity.

Several years ago, I stood next to a very tall, partially completed tower near a church in Ohio. The tower was intended to house a revolving restaurant and bring glory to God. It seems that it was also designed as a showcase for the church leaders who ordered its construction. But the funds dried up.

Jesus talked about just such a situation centuries ago. "Suppose one of you wants to build a tower. Will he not first sit down and estimate the cost to see if he has enough money to complete it? For if he lays the foundation and is not able to finish it, everyone who sees it will ridicule him, saying, 'This fellow began to build and was not able to finish.'"[25]

People who mismanage money, like the tower builders, are not likely to be effective difference makers. If you need help in dealing with finances, do what I do. Go to someone who has expertise in this area and get the guidance that you need. When our finances are in order, we are better able to make a difference, with credibility.

4. *Never stop learning.* Within the past decade, we have become a nation of physical fitness buffs. We jog, do aerobics, swim, diet, ride bicycles, lift weights, go to fitness clubs, and try to keep our bodies in shape. All of this is a healthy change from the days when exercise was avoided like the plague. Some jester has commented, however, that many people restrict their exercise to those parts of the body that are below the neck. Every muscle gets exercise, but not the brain.

In his analysis of business failures, Philip Crosby concluded that in every case the problems came because employees and executives were unwilling to keep learning or to recognize reality. "The business desert is layered with the bones of those who felt they understood completely and stopped learning."[26]

Much study can weary the body at times,[27] but this is no excuse to cut off the flow of information and new ideas into our brains. Nobody—executive, pastor, teacher, student, professional, homemaker, performer, scientist, senior citizen, musician, book writer, business person—is likely to be a relevant and genuinely effective difference maker if he or she stops learning.

5. *Follow the biblical mandate for success.* Joshua inherited a big responsibility when he took over following the death of Moses. The nation had never known another leader and Joshua wanted to be successful in his new role. God's instructions to Joshua seem strange in our age of success

books and seminars. "Be strong and courageous," Joshua was told, and recognize that "the LORD your God will be with you wherever you go." Obey the Word of God, meditate on it, and do what is written in it, "then you will be prosperous and successful."[28]

The Bible gives many guidelines for living and succeeding in this life, but perhaps the principles are summed up in this message to Joshua: Remember that God is near to give you strength, so determine to know his Word and obey his commands.

Different Kinds of Difference Makers

In the pages that have gone before, we have looked at a variety of difference makers. Some are famous; most are not. Some, like Joshua, are biblical people and historical figures; more are present-day individuals. Many realize that they are difference makers; perhaps many more do not. Some have been intent on making a difference that would honor God; others don't have that concern.

If you have not done this already, the time has come to ask yourself three basic questions:

‡ What am I doing now to make a difference?
‡ How can I make a difference in the future?
‡ What are my reasons for wanting to make a difference?

The last question may be the hardest for you to answer. Sometimes we want to make a difference so we can feel good inside, leave the world a better place in which to live, sense that our lives have done something useful, or find approval from others. In themselves, perhaps none of these are bad. Probably all of them can motivate us, at least a little.

But ultimately there is not much value in making a difference unless we are intent upon pleasing and bringing honor to God. The most lasting and valuable difference making is that which is done to bring glory to God and to his son Jesus Christ.

Make up your mind to be a difference maker—for God.

Chapter Highlights

‡ Missionaries and other international travelers are not the only people who make a lasting difference in this world. We can be difference makers even if we rarely leave our own neighborhoods.

‡ Effective difference makers often have a passion; a central life purpose that guides their activities and keeps them going.

‡ For many of us routine work, distractions, unexpected interruptions, or too many demands can hinder our effectiveness and keep us from being difference makers.

‡ Personal ambition can prevent us from being difference makers, but unselfish ambition can be a positive force that helps us reach worthy goals and become effective difference makers.

‡ Effective difference makers choose good mentors and seek to be good mentors to others.

‡ To be an effective difference maker in your neighborhood or at your place of work, seek to follow five principles: build good relationships, strive for quality, handle finances effectively, never stop learning, and follow the biblical mandate for success.

‡ Make up your mind to be a difference maker—for God.

16

Unusual Difference Makers

Sheets of cold rain driven by strong northerly winds beat against the face of the solitary figure as he made his way along the rocks, not far from the sea. It was still summer in the Scottish Highlands, mid-August, but the weather was cold and the wind-gusts were biting. The storm had stirred up giant waves that crashed in their fury against the boulders along the shoreline.

The man on the rocks seemed more invigorated than perturbed by the weather. Protected from the elements by a long raincoat and a shiny pair of Wellington boots, he began leaping from one bolder to the next, raising his voice in a duet with the howling wind. Anyone seeing him would have known that he was thoroughly engrossed in the exhilaration of hiking in the Highlands on a rainy summer afternoon.

Then he slipped.

His foot wedged into a narrow crevice and threw him off balance. As he fell, his head bashed into the rocks, knocking him unconscious.

Nobody knows how long he lay there in the rain, while the storm raged and the darkness fell. There was little hope for immediate rescue, not in that weather. When he regained consciousness the shivering man realized that he would die if he spent the night on that wet and windswept stony ledge. His only hope was to pull his leg out of its rocky vise and try to make his way back to the guest house where he had been staying.

The pain was excruciating, and when he freed his leg, it dangled, useless, like a string of limp spaghetti. Crying out to God for help, the man started the long journey back. By sitting on his coat, putting his arms behind him, and flexing the good leg, he was able to move backwards a few inches at a time up over the rocks and toward the meadow. After every twelve pushes, he would rest and pray and call out for help.

"Don't give up, Lloyd," an inaudible voice seemed to be saying in his brain. "Don't give up."

And he didn't.

Soaked to the skin and shivering in the cold, he inched his way backwards through the gooey mud and dung of a field where he was watched by unmoving, curious sheep. The pain was almost unbearable. Cuts and bruises on his weakened body added to the agony. He drifted in and out of consciousness as he slithered along, but periodically he would think of a Bible verse that he had memorized many years before. "'For I know the plans I have for you,' declares the LORD, 'plans to prosper you and not to harm you, plans to give you hope and a future.'"[1]

Even though the man couldn't have known it at the time, the Lord had a future for him. He was found in the field by a Christian physician who was taking a walk with his two daughters after the rain had stopped. Soon the injured hiker was given a shot of morphine, gently lifted into an ambulance, and driven to a hospital.

"I had run in the fast lane at top speed for years," he wrote later. "Even study times ... were round-the-clock work periods. And brief vacations were simply to catch my breath so I could start running again. Now I couldn't even walk! But still the Lord kept reminding me, 'I have plans for you ... a future and a hope.'"

The man who fell in the Highlands was an American, author of numerous books, nationally renowned preacher, and senior pastor of First Presbyterian Church in Hollywood, California. Dr. Lloyd John Ogilvie had gone to

Scotland to write a book about hope. Much of the work had been completed when he went on the fateful walk that taught him about hope first hand.[2]

He also learned about difference makers. Lloyd Ogilvie had made a difference in thousands of lives before his accident, but during the long months of recovery he learned how other caring, sensitive people could make a difference in his life. And he learned how an accident and lengthy recuperation could mold him into a more sensitive, effective, and hope-inspiring difference maker.

Unusual Difference Makers

In the pages of this book, we have seen how people living ordinary lives can be difference makers. Sometimes, however, God in his wisdom reaches down and selects a few individuals to make a unique and highly significant difference in the lives of others. These rare servants of God make up his special forces, an elite cadre of divinely appointed difference makers.

Abraham, Nehemiah, Esther, David, Daniel, Paul— these were all used by God in a special way. Mother Teresa, Billy Graham, Jim Dobson, Tom Landry, Charles Colson, Sandi Patti, Lloyd Ogilvie—these are among the people whom God has chosen to be his special difference makers in our day.

Many of these believers appear to be specially gifted with talent, resources, or opportunities. Abraham was unusually wealthy. Solomon was the wisest of all men who ever lived. Joseph and Daniel had positions of great responsibility. Esther was a queen; David was a king. Deborah was a prophetess, a military leader, and a poet in a culture dominated by men.[3] Paul was highly educated. Aquila and Priscilla were an unusually effective husband-wife team who were involved in missions, teaching, hospitality, and service in the early church.

The God who most often uses ordinary people to be difference makers also uses individuals who have unusual vision, capabilities, creativity, commitment, training, prominence, or wealth. Sometimes, he brings more resources to people so that these newly empowered individuals can have a special impact.

Only God knows why he raises some dedicated people into positions of prominence and influence, while other equally dedicated believers remain relatively unknown and unacclaimed. We do know, however, that God is most inclined to lift up those who are humble, close to him, obedient, and dedicated to being servants.[4]

Thirty years ago, A. W. Tozer wrote some insightful words about leadership that could apply equally well to difference making. You might want to read the following paragraph slowly, substituting "difference maker" for "leader" as you read.

> A true and safe leader is likely to be one who has no desire to lead, but is forced into a position of leadership by the inward pressure of the Holy Spirit and the press of the external situation. Such were Moses and David and the Old Testament prophets. I think there was hardly a great leader from Paul to the present day but was drafted by the Holy Spirit for the task, and commissioned by the Lord of the Church to fill a position he [or she] had little heart for. I believe it might be accepted as a fairly reliable rule of thumb that the man [or woman] who is ambitious to lead is disqualified as a leader. The true leader will have no desire to lord it over God's heritage, but will be humble, gentle, self-sacrificing, and altogether as ready to follow as to lead, when the Spirit makes it clear that a wiser and more gifted . . . [person] has appeared.[5]

There is nothing wrong with wanting to be a special difference maker, but God seems to place unique difference-maker responsibilities on individuals who are "humble, gentle, self-sacrificing, and altogether as ready to follow as to lead."

Innovative Difference Makers

When you were in grade school, can you ever remember a teacher telling some member of the class to "stop dreaming and pay attention"? Especially on balmy spring days, young minds can easily drift from lessons in English or mathematics to dream about more pleasant experiences out in the sunshine with friends.

Wandering minds come to all of us when we are bored, but dreaming about interesting possibilities can be stimulating, especially if we have others who help us dream. I have several very creative friends whose minds are always alive with innovative ways for making a difference. When I meet with any one of these individuals, we bounce ideas off each other—sometimes for hours—and come away exhilarated, enthusiastic, and ready to try new things. As we talk, fresh and creative ideas emerge that we hadn't thought of on our own. After our periodic meetings we go our separate ways, but our minds don't stop. Often we keep mulling over our conversation, thinking about what could be done to make a difference and how our goals could be achieved.

Some people are more creative than others. Perhaps this is something inborn, but there is evidence that creativity can be learned. It certainly can be developed, especially in people who are willing to keep learning, are inclined to discuss their ideas with others, and are not afraid to try new things.

In his study of peak performers, Charles Garfield found that some people are innovators, some are consolidators, and a few are both. Profitable companies and effective organizations, including churches, need all three. All three can be difference makers.

Innovators read widely, love to hear about breakthroughs and social trends, are interested in other people, and are concerned about politics. They expect surprises, get bored with too much routine, and seem to be energized by change and challenge. These are individuals who enjoy new ideas and delight in discussing creative possibilities with their friends. Like all creative people, innovators think in fresh and original ways. Often they notice possibilities and see things that others miss. Sometimes, however, innovators aren't able to bring their creative dreams down to reality. They have big plans, but they can't always get things done.

Consolidators, in contrast, take what is known and make things happen. These people have little interest in change, remote possibilities, or new breakthroughs. At their best, they like to do their jobs well and keep improving efficiency and competence. At their worst, they get caught up in tightly controlling the way things are done. As a result, they sometimes squelch creativity.

Most people operate between these two extremes. Sometimes we swing toward one; then we move to the other. A few rare individuals, however, seem to be skilled in both areas. They are innovators who think of bright new ideas and consolidators who know how to turn their dreams into reality. Innovators and consolidators working together often make the greatest difference.

When our family was living in Switzerland, my wife and I visited L'Abri Fellowship. In a small village surrounded by mountains, Francis and Edith Schaeffer led a Christian community of individuals, families, travelers, spiritual seekers, and students who lived, worked, shared, learned, and worshiped together. After lunch on the day of our visit, Dr. Francis Schaeffer spoke informally and answered a few questions.

We had read many of his books and listened to some of his tapes, but it was inspiring and informative for us to watch this dedicated Bible scholar interact with the people at L'Abri. He was an avid reader, a brilliant philosopher, a renowned theologian, and a fine speaker who could be sensitive and highly insightful. Especially toward the end of his life, Dr. Schaeffer was used by God as a world-wide difference maker. His writings were widely read, his lectures were well attended, and his films were pioneering educational efforts.[6]

Francis Schaeffer constantly interacted with people, kept aware of the world through his travel and reading, and was willing to risk trying things that were new. Apparently he was a both an innovator and a consolidator. He was a humble man, available to be used by God. He was a special difference maker.

Several years ago, Francis Schaeffer's earthly pilgrimage ended when cancer snuffed out his life. But his influence continues. In many ways he was a model for those who sense that they could be touched by God to be his innovative difference makers.

Visionary Difference Makers

God's special difference makers are not always innovators, but invariably they are people of vision.

Vision has been called "the key to achieving great impact for God"; the one characteristic that "makes the difference" in the lives of Christians who want to be difference makers.

Vision separates people who are in the middle of the action from those who are watching from the sidelines. George Barna defined vision as "the difference between floundering in uncertainty and moving ahead in the assurance of God's leading and purpose."[7]

Vision is described by Warren Bennis as "the first basic ingredient of leadership," the "most pivotal" of all the characteristics that outstanding leaders possess.[8] In his classic book on spiritual leadership, J. Oswald Sanders wrote that "those who have most powerfully and permanently influenced their generation have been men [and women] who have seen more and further than others."[9] Sanders argues effectively that the great missionary pioneers, without exception, were people of vision—individuals who could look beyond present problems and see future possibilities and potential.

According to the chairman of General Motors, vision is the place where the art of management begins, "a quality that has never been so crucial as it is today."[10]

Vision is frequently present in God's special difference makers.

What do we mean by vision?

There are different definitions[11] but they all suggest that a *vision* is the clear sense of knowing where you are going with your life, career, and ministry. It is a sense of direction, a driving force, a determination to reach some goal despite setbacks, fatigue, opposition, discouragement, or even periodic failures. It is similar to the passion that we considered in the preceding chapter, but vision is broader. It encompasses all of life and involves both a deep commitment to some task and a decisive, sometimes evolving, plan of action. Vision includes optimism and hope, the ability to see potential when others see only obstacles and impossibilities.

Look at Christian visionaries, suggests George Barna, and you will find men and women with four characteristics. First, they are people of *prayer*, who continually seek God's guidance and listen for his leading. Second, visionaries are people of *action*. When they are fired up by a need that is going unmet, they seek God's direction and provision, plan step by step ways to meet the need, enlist the help of others, and move ahead. Third, visionaries are people of *perseverance*. They expect to encounter setbacks and opposition but they are unshakable in their resolve to do what they feel God is leading them to do. At times the task may seem overwhelming, but they are like Paul who wrote that he had no choice but to preach the Gospel. The love of Christ compelled him to continue his ministry.[12] Visionary people have a similar compelling determination to reach their goals. Fourth, people with vision are people of *excitement*. They radiate a zeal and sense of purpose. Often they feel that their lives are on the cutting edge, blazing new and uncharted territory.[13]

There are many visionaries in the Bible, but there is no better example than Nehemiah who had a vision for rebuilding the walls around Jerusalem and, despite intense opposition, stuck with the task until the job was finished.

As we have seen, many effective difference makers are not visionaries. But if you are one of those who seems to have the potential to be a visionary or if you are motivated by one or more life visions, ask God to show you an area of need that can be met with your interests, talents, and abilities. Learn all you can about the issue or issues that concern you. It is a great waste of time, energy, and resources to launch into a project without knowing what is needed, what others have done or are doing, what skills and provisions will be necessary for moving toward your goal. Pray at every step of the way. Enlist the help, input, and talents of others. Ministries and projects that are launched by one person and built around one leader frequently get off track and end up in disaster. Be prepared for difficulties, perhaps even persecution, because these come to visionaries who are intent on making a difference.[14]

How does all of this affect you?

Do the above paragraphs sound like something you could do, or do they seem to be describing somebody else? It is easy to be overwhelmed when we read about visionaries. Each of us can feel that "this is for others and not for me." If your reading has stirred up this kind of reaction— which is very common—try to remember two things.

First, visionaries are not always high-profile people who are determined to change the world. God gives big visions to a few people, who in turn have major responsibilities, frequently accompanied by major difficulties. More often, however, God gives us much smaller, more manageable visions—like influencing family members, giving love and Kool Aid to the latchkey kids on the street, or encouraging missionaries with letters and prayer. These are less prominent but no less important. Only people judge by numbers, size, and appearances. God is more concerned with faithfulness, obedience, and excellence.[15]

Second, while everybody can be a difference maker it seems that only some people are visionaries. Consider Nehemiah. He had a God-inspired vision for rebuilding the protective walls around Jerusalem and he gave overall direction to the task. Think of the chaos that would have ensued if everybody had been equally visionary. When Nehemiah surveyed the destroyed walls of the city, he had the overarching vision to rebuild; others worked diligently as part of the team.

Powerful Difference Makers

When Michael Korda wrote *Power! How to Get It, How to Use It*, his book quickly became a bestseller.[16] Writing in a provocative, no-nonsense style, the author argued that life is a game of power: getting it, controlling it, and using it to obtain security, fame, sex, and money. After quoting Lord Acton's famous statement that "Power tends to corrupt and absolute power corrupts absolutely," Korda argued that it is worse to not push for power. We live in a world that is run by power, he wrote, and we need to grab it, hang on to it, enjoy it, and use it to get what we want.

Everybody knows about power struggles between husbands and wives, parents and children, rival street gangs, political foes, and opposing factions in universities, corporations, professional organizations, religious denominations, or churches. Most of these struggles involve self-centered actions, hard-feelings, anger, and the manipulation of other people. The players in the power games feel anxiety and insecurity, even when they win the largest share of the power.

It is not easy to be a difference maker in a world, a community, or a family where people are struggling for power. Sometimes, we have to work with individuals (often incompetent and unreasonable individuals) who are jealous of their power and threatened when they learn about our difference-maker plans and passions. At times we must work within the power conscious system of local government. We may have to get approval for our buildings and plans from committees, church boards, or people in positions of power. Sometimes it seems difficult to maintain integrity when we have to live and work in a power-crazed culture. According to futurist Alvin Toffler, we are entering a period of history when "the entire structure of power that held the world together is now disintegrating." There is a major power shift taking place, says Toffler. It stretches from the highest levels of government to the daily interactions we have with our neighbors, family members, and colleagues at work. As this century ends, it seems that everybody will experience sometimes radical changes in who holds power, how it is used, and how it is controlled.[17]

Despite these changes, however, we are not helpless pawns in the hands of others who hold power or struggle to get it. For centuries, committed and determined difference makers have been able to make significant changes, despite the power of others who get in the way. When God is leading us to make a difference, we can move forward with confidence, especially when we remember two important truths: power can be destructive, but ultimate power belongs to God.

Power can be destructive. Too often power is misused. What results is not good. According to Richard Foster, power often destroys relationships, trust, dialogue, and integrity.

"The sin of the garden was the sin of power. They wanted to be more, to have more, to know more than is right. Not content to be creatures, they wanted to be gods." When power and pride go together, writes Foster, we have the most destructive force of all, especially when the pride and power reside in people who have no accountability.[18]

Back in the sixth century there were many wandering prophets and monks who looked pious, spoke eloquently, and were widely acclaimed by the Christian communities where they visited. These itinerant preachers had power, pride, and arrogance, but they had no accountability. As a result, many of them fell into sinful, self-indulgent corruption.

Something similar can happen to modern preachers and other believers who wield power, even limited power, but aren't accountable to anyone except themselves. Jim Bakker's extravagant spending, naïve belief that God would continue to provide for his enterprises, and policy of creating new projects to pay for the old ones led to a ministry-edifice that had to collapse. He was a man with power and pride, but he had no real accountability.

Is it surprising that Satan's forces are called "the powers of this dark world?"[19] On the day that I began this chapter, I pulled away in the evening to attend the midweek worship service at a nearby church. The message that night was about Daniel, but at one point the speaker paused and made a statement that riveted my attention. "I'm not sure I can prove this scripturally," he said, "but there seems to be abundant evidence that *the more we are concerned about making a difference, the more Satan and the powers of darkness are active in creating problems and raising obstacles.*"[20]

How do we defeat these satanic powers and make a difference in our power-hungry society?[21]

First, we recognize that Christ has already defeated the powers of darkness. In his death and resurrection he "disarmed the powers and authorities, he made a public spectacle of them, triumphing over them by the cross."[22] The Holy Spirit who lives in us is greater than the Devil and satanic power in the world.[23]

Second, with the Holy Spirit's guidance and strength, we must refuse to play power games. We don't try to dominate, intimidate, or manipulate people and circumstances to get what we want. We constantly look at our own motives and seek to be free of the lust for money, sex, control, and power.

Third, we must keep accountable to God and to Christian friends who can pray for us, encourage us, challenge us, point to our blind spots, call us to change, and expect that we will live God-pleasing lives. We realize that the Holy Spirit, living within believers, brings about change so we need not play the world's manipulation and power games. We must be men and women who are walking with God on a daily basis, employing all the weapons of Ephesians 6:10–18.

With God's help, we can rise above the destructive grip of earthly power—even shifting earthly power—and become uniquely effective difference makers.

Ultimate power belongs to God. When he walked on earth, Jesus probably didn't look very powerful. For a time he chose to not use his power, but at the end of his life he told the disciples that *all* power and authority, in heaven and in earth, is under his control.[24]

For a while Satan has some of the power, but he won't keep it. Satan's power is on loan. Even though he presently uses that power to roam the earth like a roaring lion looking for people to devour, he won't remain powerful forever.[25]

When Jesus sent the twelve disciples on a short training mission, he gave them instructions, told them what to expect, and modeled for them what they were supposed to do. But before they went out, the disciples also received power and authority from Jesus to make a difference for God.[26]

That power is still available. It is not a power that depends on position, money, education, or the people we know. It is not power that is used to advance our reputations, strengthen our careers, fill our pockets, impress others, or inflate our egos.

God's power involves servanthood, submission, and humility. It is seen in people whose lives are characterized by a growing love, joy, peace, patience, kindness, goodness, faithfulness, gentleness, and self-control.[27] The Bible radically challenges almost everything that Michael Korda wrote in his best-selling book about power. The Scriptures make the incredible statement that we have the greatest strength and power when we are weak.[28] It is then that Christ's ultimate power rests upon us and enables us to be his special difference makers.

A powerful revolution. Historians in the future will surely look back to 1989 as one of the revolutionary years that changed the world. Within a few months, almost all of Eastern Europe rose up in revolt against a communist system that had dominated and subjugated millions since the 1940s. It was mostly a nonviolent revolution. It was largely a spiritual revolution when the power of communism crumbled in response to the power of prayer.

In communist East Germany, for example, the party promoted atheism but the faith of the people survived. Within church walls many found hope, sanctuary, and relief from the bleak realities of state communism. Every Monday night churches all over the land held prayer meetings. Initially attendance was small but it continued to grow until it reached into the hundreds. Then there were thousands, sometimes overflowing into the streets.

Often the people carried candles, symbols of hope. Some called 1989 a revolution of prayer and candles. "We have candle wax in our streets instead of blood," one man said joyfully after the Berlin wall fell. There were no party caucuses, no magnetic liberators, no riots, no angry confrontations with tanks and gunfire. The people, instead, emerged from their prayer meetings, rose up, and demanded change. Ironically, Erich Honecker, the shamed and dying autocrat who had almost destroyed his own homeland, could only find refuge in the home of a Lutheran pastor. The church that the communist leader had tried to destroy became his haven.

"What happened in East Germany should remind us that people who believe in an idea are still the most powerful source, humanly speaking, in history," observed James R. Edwards. All of us who want to be difference makers should remember that the way things are is not the way things must always be. Before God, the nations with all their power "are regarded by him as worthless and less than nothing. . . . He brings princes to naught and reduces the rulers of this world to nothing." All power still belongs to him.[29]

Competent Difference Makers

On the way to becoming a psychologist I enrolled in some good graduate schools. I received excellent training, read hundreds of up-to-date journal articles, had a valuable internship, got experience in a variety of practical settings, and learned from some fine faculty members and practicum supervisors. I passed the required examinations, became licensed as a clinical psychologist, and am legally qualified to open a private practice where I probably could make a difference as a counselor.

There is evidence, however, that most of what I learned in graduate school is now out of date. The same would be true if I had chosen to be an engineer, physician, lawyer, stock broker, military officer, mechanic, fire-fighter, farmer, or worker in almost any other field. What we learn during the course of our training soon becomes outdated. If we aren't active in keeping up, our knowledge becomes obsolete and we become largely incompetent.

In an age when people write about excellence, integrity, commitment, quality, innovation, creativity, and passion, it seems surprising that few say much about competence. People who are competent have the skills, know-how, and experience to do what they do with a sense of mastery. Sir Yehudi Menuhin is a competent violinist. Billy Graham is a competent evangelist. Frances Schaeffer was a competent scholar.

I suspect, however, that genuine competence is rare. Perhaps some people give up trying to keep up when they are surrounded by the swirl of rapid change that can leave all of us so quickly out of date. Others are incompetent because they are unwilling, too busy, or too lazy to develop and maintain mastery of their fields. Some people don't try to be competent because they can get along just fine the way they are. I once knew an elderly, dedicated church treasurer who refused to use computers or modern bookkeeping methods because the techniques he learned fifty years ago still seemed to do the job. Nobody wanted to hurt his feelings by suggesting that he was both outdated and incompetent. I cringe at the thought of how many professors I have known who get tenure and continue to teach their classes but don't bother to learn anything new. They are well paid and professionally incompetent.

Isn't it amazing that God often uses incompetent people to be difference makers? Earlier we were reminded that those who are wise, influential, or noble rarely get called into Christian service. Perhaps these people are too proud to serve or to learn. Paul, himself, had a number of weaknesses, but God made him competent.[30] Christian difference makers all stumble and make mistakes, especially at the beginning, but the Lord enables them to become competent.

In the pages of this book we have seen repeatedly that God uses people who are not very competent. But sometimes he reaches down and selects people who develop an unusually high degree of competence. These are talented people who give of themselves fully, practice continually, and strive shamelessly to develop the highest possible levels of proficiency and expertise. In part because of this practice and devotion, these people become uniquely capable and highly effective difference makers.

Daniel was one of these people. Shortly after the Babylonian armies besieged Jerusalem and captured a group of exiles, the king of Babylon called in the chief of his court officials and issued an order. "Bring in some of the Israelites from the royal family and the nobility—young men without any physical defect, handsome, showing aptitude for every kind of learning, well informed, quick to understand, and qualified to serve in the king's palace." The monarch wanted these young men to learn the language and literature of Babylon. They were to be groomed for positions of responsibility in the kingdom.

Daniel was one of the young men—historians suggest that they were probably teenagers—who were chosen. "God gave knowledge and understanding of all kinds of literature and learning," to these choice servants, the Bible tells us. They were able to understand visions and dreams. When the king questioned them after their training, he discovered that they were "ten times better than all the magicians and enchanters in his whole kingdom." Maybe the king didn't know that Daniel and his colleagues were also godly young men who prayed consistently, humbled themselves before God, and were not afraid to let their beliefs be known.[31]

Daniel was unusually gifted to begin with, but he

devoted himself to becoming increasingly competent in his service to the royal household. During his lifetime he did his job effectively under three different kings and made a powerful difference in their lives and in the life of the kingdom.

Daniel so distinguished himself among the other leaders of the land that they became jealous and tried to find grounds for charges against him. But according to the Bible, they "could find no corruption in him, because he was trustworthy and neither corrupt nor negligent." Only then did the royal officials concoct the scheme that led to Daniel's meeting with the hungry lions.[32]

Almost everybody knows the story of Daniel in the lion's den—how God protected him from harm. Fewer people are aware of Daniel's consistent prayer life, his walk with God, and his ability to give thanks even when he knew that he might die because of his faith.[33]

Daniel was one of God's choice difference makers. As a young man he was chosen by God; then he spent a lifetime developing competence and walking with his Lord.

How does that apply to us? Very few people have been born in a royal family and given the opportunities that came to Daniel. Few of us are as intelligent, as educated, or as close to prominent people. But we can all seek to be as competent as possible—in our work, our marriage building and parenting, our places of service, and our walking with God. He can help us to become more competent as servants and as difference makers, regardless of our backgrounds and innate capabilities.[34]

Patient Difference Makers

A year or so before the first Christmas morning, an elderly priest named Zechariah was visited by an angel. Luke wrote that Zechariah and his wife Elizabeth were "upright in the sight of God, observing all the Lord's commandments and regulations blamelessly." They must have prayed for children, but they were childless and socially scorned as a result. Imagine their reaction, then, when the angel declared that Elizabeth would bear a son who would make an extraordinary difference in the world.

Six months later, a young relative of Elizabeth, a woman named Mary, also was visited by an angel whose message was even more startling. Even though she was a virgin, Mary would become the mother of God's Son, the long-awaited Messiah.

It isn't surprising that the younger woman hurried across the hill country to the town where Elizabeth lived and together they waited for the first of these miracle children to be born.[35]

I wonder if it was hard to wait?

Waiting is not easy. Waiting patiently is harder still.

Elizabeth, like Sarah before her, had waited a whole lifetime for God to give her a child. Abraham waited for one hundred years before he became the father of a promised son. Moses was eighty before he was called for special service. Joseph was cast into prison for a crime he never committed, and he waited for a long time before God used him as a difference maker. John the Baptist, Elizabeth's son, waited in the wilderness before he was used to announce the coming of the Messiah. We don't know how long the father waited for the Prodigal Son to come home. Saul of Tarsus, God's "chosen instrument," waited before he began his active ministry. After he got started, part of his life was spent in prison waiting for the opportunity to get on with the work that he felt called to do.

Mother Teresa waited over two years to be released from her vows so she could start the work that led, eventually, to the Nobel Peace Prize. The persecuted people of Eastern Europe waited over forty years to be liberated from communist oppression.

And Lloyd Ogilvie waited.

Even as he was lifted into the ambulance after his brush with death in the Highlands, the pastor from California protested. "Where are you sending me?" he asked in his weakened voice. "Can't you fix my leg here, give me some crutches, and send me on my way?" The long months of recuperation were not easy, especially for a man who was in the middle of writing a book about hope and the future.

Waiting is hard because we want to get into the action and on with the job. But waiting helps to mold us and prepare us for future service. Abraham, Elizabeth, John the Baptist, Mary, and others were able to wait because they believed that what the Lord said would be accomplished. They were willing to be the Lord's servants and difference makers—in accordance with his timing.[36]

To wait expectantly, knowing that God is in control, is an unusual attitude toward life. "The spiritual life is a life in which we wait," Henri Nouwen wrote, "trusting that new things will happen to us, new things that are far beyond our own imagination, fantasy, or prediction. That, indeed, is a very radical stance toward life in a world preoccupied with control."[37]

And how do we respond if God chooses us to be among his uniquely used group of difference makers? How do we react if he touches us, but then lets us wait? Mary yielded her life to God and praised him for his goodness.[38] Then she waited.

The world is filled with people who want to be difference makers. Most will make a difference in quiet ways. Some might be innovators, visionaries, or people with power and great competence. Some are already making a difference; others discover that they must wait a while longer.

When Lloyd Ogilvie was fully recovered, someone asked how he was going to spend the rest of his life. There was no hesitation in his response. He would draw on God's limitless resources, "every moment, and run with Him on two strong legs."

The Lord has plans for you and me. We have hope and a future. And we can be difference makers. But for a while, we may have to wait.

Chapter Highlights

‡ Most of the world's difference makers are ordinary people living ordinary lives. But sometimes in his wisdom God reaches down and selects a few individuals to make unique and highly significant differences in the lives of others.

‡ These unusual or special difference makers are often innovative, able to get things done, and visionary. Many make a powerful impact. Some are unusually competent.

‡ Visionary difference makers are people of prayer, action, perseverance, and excitement—individuals who radiate zeal and a sense of purpose. But visionaries are not always high-profile people who are determined to change the world.

‡ We live in a world of shifting power. Such power can be destructive and annoying, but ultimately all power belongs to God. Even Satan's power is limited.

‡ God's power most often comes to people who are servants, submissive, and humble.

‡ Some difference makers are not especially competent, but God enables others to become highly competent.

‡ To be a difference maker for God often involves periods of waiting. Such waiting is not easy. Waiting patiently is harder still.

17

You Can Be a
Difference Maker

There were howls of protest when the students got the news.

A quarter of the senior class signed a petition of complaint.

Many were angered that the administration of a prestigious women's college should select a commencement speaker whose fame was due to her husband's success and not the result of her own achievements.

The incident attracted national attention and raised the ire of many women, especially full-time mothers who felt that they were being insulted by the student protests. Columnist Erma Bombeck, known for her humor, became unusually serious and firmly advised the complaining students to go back to class. "You're not ready to graduate yet," she wrote. "You've got a lot to learn."

And how did the invited speaker respond?

Barbara Bush graciously and courageously accepted the invitation and spoke to the graduating class of Wellesley, a highly regarded women's college in Massachusetts. She even brought a friend, Raisa Gorbachev, wife of the Soviet leader, who was visiting the United States at the time.

In her commencement address, Mrs. Bush acknowledged that she was not the first choice for many of the students, but she went on to talk about more important choices in the future. "I hope many of you will consider making three very special choices," she said.

"The first is to believe in something larger than yourself, to get involved in some of the big ideas of our time." Mrs.

Bush chose literacy—long before her husband began his quest for the White House. She knew that teaching people to read and write would be a significant way to make a difference in thousands of lives—and indirectly in the nation and society.

The second choice may seem less noble at first, but it is no less important. "Early on, I made another choice, which I hope you will make as well," the first lady continued. "Whether you are talking about education, career, or service, you are talking about life, and life must really have joy. It's supposed to be fun."

The third choice, Mrs. Bush indicated, "is to cherish your human connections, your relationships with family and friends." Building careers can be important and fulfilling, she acknowledged, but "you are a human being first, and those human connections with spouses, with children, with friends are the most important investment you will ever make. At the end of your life, you will never regret not having passed one more test, not winning one more verdict, or not closing one more deal. You *will* regret time not spent with your husband, a child, a friend, or a parent. . . . Your success . . . our success as a society, depends not on what happens in the White House, but on what happens inside your house."

Perhaps with a twinkle in her eye, the first lady finished her speech with some words of encouragement. "Who knows? Somewhere out in this audience may even be someone who will one day follow in my footsteps and preside over the White House as the President's spouse . . . I wish him well!"

Where Have We Been?

Mrs. Bush was talking about making a difference even though she never used those words in her commencement address.

Difference makers are often people who choose to devote their lives and energies to causes that are bigger than themselves. They choose to make the best of life, even when things are difficult, and they look for ways to find joy in the journey. Difference makers often work hard at their careers, but they know that life can be empty when there are no deep and lasting relationships with family and friends.

The desk where I write is near a window through which I can see a small flower garden. During the weeks that I have been working on this book, my gaze has often gone to that little plot of ground and I have watched the changes in the plants as they have gone through the summer months. The spring tulips and daffodils lost their foliage and the leaves turned brown a long time ago. The deep purple irises have been replaced by bright red geraniums, brilliant yellow marigolds, pink and white impatiens, and multicolored lilies. Soon the lily blossoms will be gone for this year, but the late summer salvia and zinnias are beginning to show their splendor—until the coming of the fall chrysanthemums. Some day, probably in October, the frosts will come, the plants will all wither, and my garden plot will be bare once again, waiting for the winter snow.

I am not the best gardener; my flowers don't do equally well. Some grow tall, brilliant in color, visible from a distance. Many are small and less eye-catching. A few, like the lilies that I see as I write, are past their prime, with petals that are fading in color and likely to drop soon. Many of my plants are so tiny that they are almost unnoticeable. Others, overshadowed by taller plants, are struggling to get into the sun and out from under the domination of their more powerful garden neighbors. A few of my plants look like they are gasping to keep alive. Some have already died.

In our journey through these pages we have seen difference makers who are like those garden plants. Some are prominent and highly visible; others are hardly noticed. Many are healthy; others are not. Some are just beginning to bloom; great numbers are past their prime. A few seem to be struggling to get out from under the shadow of another; many are at the peak of their brilliance and productivity. Some are gasping to keep alive. Others have already died. And in time, all will be gone.

Then what will be left?

Will your life have made a lasting difference, or will it have been alive for a while, even blossomed, and then passed from the scene like my fading flowers in the fall?

Difference makers, as we have seen, come in all shapes, sizes, skills, and styles of influence. Because of these variations, it is hard to define what we mean by a difference maker, but perhaps in this last chapter we can offer a tentative definition. *A difference maker is an individual whose attitudes, values, and actions encourage, free, equip, teach, help, or in some other way benefit the lives of others.* The difference maker's influence can be brief, or it may last for a long time.

In the preceding pages we have seen that some people make a splendid and significant difference in the world, but more often difference makers are people doing ordinary things to touch the lives of others. The book of Hebrews gives an inspiring gallery of men and women of faith; we have seen something similar in the lives of the people who have appeared in the chapters of this book.

Susanna Wesley, Carrie Ponder, and Nancy Beach's father made a difference as parents.

Churchill and Eisenhower made a difference as political leaders. So did David, Joseph, and Daniel.

Jessica Siegel, Kenneth Kantzer, Mark Hennebach, Gilbert Bilezikian, and R. C. Sproul have all made a difference as teachers.

Yehudi Menuhin, Sarah Cannon, and Tom Landry have been difference makers in the fields of entertainment.

Mr. Ninan made a difference in India by doing his duty.

Chris and Mildred Sommerfield made a difference by staying at home and praying for missionaries. Aurelia Rau taught Sunday School. Lizbeth and Gladys went into the dump. Alberta befriended a young man dying with AIDS. Jane Hill showed love to a blustery but hurting street lady.

Robert Girard made a difference by showing us how to recover after a dream vanishes. Lloyd Ogilvie showed how to wait in hope while a physical injury healed. Hoshino Tomihiro has shown us how to make a difference when physical recovery never comes.

Charles Colson, Henri Nouwen, Paul Tournier, and Francis Schaeffer with his wife, Edith, have all been effective writers, making a difference through their pens and word processors. Each of them could be linked with Albert Schweitzer, Mother Teresa, and thousands of others, unknown and unacclaimed, who work with the needy.

Kenneth Wessner represents those who make a difference in business. Lee Strobel has made a difference as a public speaker. Don Michel has made a difference in the inner city. Dave and Nancy Smith have made a difference in showing us faith. People with names like Matthews, Custis, and Finlay have shown how difference makers can have an influence through their homes. Bill Russell turned away from a lucrative law practice and is making a greater difference within his mission. Masaru Horikoshi is emerging as a difference maker in the field of psychology. And the boy rescuing starfish on that debris-strewn beach showed how each of us can make a difference by touching one small life at a time.

There are names from the earlier pages that we have not repeated here—biblical names, contemporary names, names of famous people, and names of some who would not expect to be mentioned in any book.

But this impressive parade of individual difference makers leaves us with some sobering questions.

Where would your name fit?

What kind of a difference maker are you and what could you become?

From this point on, what will you do with your life to make a difference that will last forever?

The Bible reminds us that life is like those plants in my garden. Human beings are "like grass, and all their glory is like the flowers of the field; the grass withers and the flowers fall...."[1] But unlike dead flowers that are gone forever, the Word of God lasts. So do people and their influence. "Anyone, then, who knows the good he [or she] ought to do and doesn't do it, sins."[2]

How, therefore, can we be difference makers who make a lasting impact on this world—an impact that can last forever?

Where Are We Going?

When Jesus chose the twelve disciples, did anybody consider Peter to be a poor choice? Impulsive, stubborn, poorly educated, and inclined to curse and swear when he was under pressure, Peter seemed an unlikely candidate on which to build the world's first church. Perhaps it is true that the Pharisees looked at Peter and saw only a poor unlettered fisherman, totally insignificant, not worthy of a second glance. In contrast Jesus saw in Peter, "the prophet and preacher, saint and leader of the unique band of men who turned the world upside down."[3]

What made the difference in Peter? How did he become the difference maker who preached to a great crowd on the day of Pentecost, led the early church, and wrote two powerful New Testament epistles?

After the Resurrection, when Jesus talked to Peter on the beach, the disciple was given two guidelines for living.

Peter built the rest of his life on these principles. They summarize the message of this book and they point the way for each of us who wants to become a difference maker. Jesus said "Follow me" and "Feed my sheep."[4]

Follow the Shepherd

In this world, many people are difference makers even though they have no interest in anything religious and no desire to follow Jesus Christ. With determination, hard work, practice, courage, skill, creativity, persistence, ambition, and self-motivation, mixed perhaps with a little inspiration and encouragement from others, many individuals become successful at making a difference. Some of history's greatest achievements and changes for good have come from dedicated, visionary people who are motivated to leave the world a better place than they found it.

But people who make a difference for God have a different set of priorities. They want to know God, to worship him, obey him, and become more like him. They want to wait for his leading instead of rushing into their own projects. They pray for humility, strive for integrity, live lives of purity, and never stop learning. Instead of laboring to build their own empires, they work to build people. Instead of cowering because of their failures and weaknesses, they find strength in the one who is all powerful. They confess their sins and seek to develop their God-given gifts and talents. They learn from mentors and seek to be models for others. They know their inadequacies, cultivate their special abilities, and seek to co-operate with others in a spirit of love and harmony. They work diligently in their jobs or careers, but they are devoted marriage partners who refuse to sacrifice their families on an altar that worships career success. Some difference makers are visionaries, people-helpers, gracious in showing hospitality, innovators, risk takers, individuals with passion and ambition. If they read this paragraph probably most of them would think "All of this applies to somebody else. That's not me! I'll never make it."

Like Peter, the Christ-honoring difference maker knows that he or she is weak and inclined to fail. But by the time he reached the end of his life, Peter had learned what it was like to be a Christ-follower.

"Grow in the grace and knowledge of our Lord and Savior Jesus Christ," Peter wrote in his parting message.[5]

Prepare your minds for action.

Be holy in all you do.

Love one another deeply, from the heart.

Live as servants of God.

Show proper respect for everyone.

Follow in his steps.

Live in harmony with one another.

Be prepared to give an answer to everyone who asks you to give the reason for the hope that you have.

Be clear minded and self-controlled.

Clothe yourselves with humility.

Live such good lives among the pagans that, though they accuse you of doing wrong, they may see your good deeds and glorify God.[6]

Such instructions continue throughout the apostle's two little books. Interspersed are Peter's warnings that following Christ will never be easy. Worthwhile things never are.

But following Christ and becoming an effective difference maker is possible. It takes time, patience, and a willingness to let him lead.

Feed the Sheep

On the night when Jesus was arrested, Peter denied Christ three times. Some have suggested that this is why Jesus later asked the same question three times: "Do you love me?" Each time after Peter's reply, the Lord said to feed his sheep.

Maybe by this repetition Jesus was also emphasizing that the servant of God, who loves and follows the Shepherd, must also be actively concerned about others.

A. W. Tozer once wrote about the great saints and spiritual giants of the past, but he could have been writing about modern difference makers. Spiritual leaders have often displayed glaring differences from each other, Tozer wrote, but there have been two common features in all of their lives. They have had a *spiritual receptivity* so they were open to God's leading, and they *did something about this*.[7] Stated differently, they made it their business to know and follow Christ, the Good Shepherd, and they took action to be involved with people, his sheep.

If you want to be a difference maker, spend time knowing God and he will reveal his plans for you. In time you will find yourself involved in activities that draw on your abilities and talents, that bring genuine fulfillment into your life, and that involve you with other people. Your life may show no dramatic changes, but someday you will look back and recognize, perhaps with surprise, that God has made a difference through you and that he is continuing to use you as one of his difference makers.

So Where Do We Go From Here?

Stuart Briscoe tells a story about Phillips Brooks, the powerful preacher who lived a century ago and wrote "O Little Town of Bethlehem." The great man was pacing fretfully back and forth in his office, muttering to himself, when somebody asked why he appeared so troubled.

"I'm troubled," Brooks replied, "because I'm in a hurry and God isn't!"

Do you ever feel that way? For about ten years I was at a stage in my career when I felt like a small Piper Cub sitting at the side of a busy airport runway, waiting for clearance to take off. In the meantime planes of all shapes and sizes were passing me, revving up their engines, and soaring beautifully and gracefully into the sky.

One day I reached the point of thinking that I might never take off and make a difference. "Lord," I said, "it isn't easy for an active person like me, but I'm willing to stay where I am, for all of my life if need be, sitting in a corner, willing and ready to go, while I watch others pass by with your clearance to take off and make a difference."

I can't tell you where I am today. Some days I feel like I am still on the runway, but I don't get frustrated as easily. My job is to know Christ better and remain ready to go where and when the divine control tower directs. I want him to lead, showing where and how I can be a difference maker for him.

What About You?

If you have read this far, you are minutes from finishing this book. Then what?

Will you put this copy on the shelf or maybe pass it on to someone else and then forget what you have read? Will you decide to put some of what you have read into practice but then get busy with other things and go on without making any changes in your life?

The preceding pages contain many examples of difference makers—examples of people who might be good models for us to follow. I have also tried to include reminders and suggestions to help us become more effective as difference makers. As we reach the last page, could I encourage you to pause, to pray, to ask God to show you how you can become a better difference maker? Could you skim back through the book, if necessary, and decide on one or two actions that you will take this week—maybe even today—with the help of God and the help of others? Please don't be the kind of person who reads a book about becoming a difference maker and goes away unchanged— no more of a difference maker than when you read page one.

In 1917 a man named James Montgomery Flagg painted a recruitment poster for the United States Army. Probably you have seen the picture. It shows a stern faced Uncle Sam wearing a top hat over his flowing white hair and pointing directly at the viewer. In bold letters across the bottom, the poster reads

I WANT <u>YOU</u> FOR THE U.S. ARMY.

I wonder if God has a similar message in these days of change and stress, opportunity and violence, hope and hassles? He still invites us to join the ranks of people across history who have been his difference makers. He will use those who are eager to let him lead.

Everybody who is willing to learn and to serve in the ranks of God's army *will* be a difference maker. It all depends on how you respond to his recruitment poster. It's message is simple, but it demands a response:

GOD WANTS <u>YOU</u> TO BE A
DIFFERENCE MAKER!

Chapter Highlights

‡ In the preceding pages we have seen a variety of difference makers.

‡ A difference maker is an individual whose attitudes, values, and actions encourage, free, equip, teach, help, or in some other way benefit the lives of others. The difference maker's influence can be brief or for a long time.

‡ At first the apostle Peter must have seemed like an unlikely difference maker, but he learned two lessons: to follow Christ and to feed his sheep. Following Christ and becoming one of his difference makers is possible for all believers.

‡ Each of us must decide what, specifically, we will do next to become a more effective difference maker.

‡ God wants you to be one of his difference makers.

Appendix
Doing a Life Status Check

Periodically there is value in looking at our lives to evaluate where we are, what we have accomplished, how we spend our time, where we are going, and how we might be more effective as difference makers. The following exercise might help you with that evaluation process.

Scriptural guidelines. Starting with the Bible, think about some principles for establishing priorities and making a difference. The following list is not intended to be complete. You may compile a list that is different, but start by considering the following:

‡ God gives wisdom and leading if we trust him (Proverbs 3:5–6).

‡ God gives strength if we wait on him (Isaiah 40:28-31).

‡ God knows us, purges wrong motives and sinful actions from our lives, and leads us (Psalm 139:23–24).

‡ God expects us to plan, but he guides our steps (Proverbs 16:9).

‡ Our lives are not our own; we don't direct our own steps (Jeremiah 10:23).

‡ God has plans for his people. He gives us hope for the future (Jeremiah 29:11).

‡ God gives us success in response to our prayers and when we live in obedience to him and in accordance to his plans (Genesis 24; Joshua 1).

‡ God expects us to please him (2 Corinthians 5:9).

‡ God's love, experiencing it and sharing it, must be our chief motivator (John 13:34–35; 2 Corinthians 5:14)

Looking at your activities. For a few minutes write answers to four basic questions: What do I do best? What do I do okay? What do I have to do, even though I don't like it? What is the best use of my time?

When you get your answers, look over the list and then show it to some person who knows you well.

How would your list change in light of this discussion?

Evaluating your activities. Take a sheet of paper and draw eleven columns. The column on the left should be about two inches wide, the others can be more narrow.

1. In the wide column on the left, list all of your activities: present, coming, and possible.

2. At the top of the next nine columns write in the first nine letters of the alphabet.

3. In the column at the far right, write *Totals*. The paper should look like this:

Activities	a	b	c	d	e	f	g	h	i	Totals

4. The following questions parallel each of the above letters. For example, "a" above stands for question "a" below.
   a. Does this activity build Christ's kingdom?
   b. Does this help and/or build up others?
   c. Does this make maximum use of my spiritual gifts?
   d. Will this strengthen the church?
   e. Does this contribute to my spiritual growth?
   f. Does this bring honor to Christ?
   g. Is this of crucial significance?
   h. Does this meet my personal and family needs?
   i. Do I enjoy doing this?

5. Each of the activities that you have listed in column one should be given a number of 0 to 5, with 0 being the strongest possible "no" and 5 being the strongest "yes."

6. Rank the activities one at a time and put the totals in the column at the far right. The following is an example. (You, of course, might assign different numbers to each of the activities.)

Activities	a	b	c	d	e	f	g	h	i	Totals
"Teaching Sunday school"	4	4	3	5	3	4	3	0	5	31
"Taking an evening class"	2	3	4	4	2	3	4	5	5	32

7. Now look over your list and the total tally. Since you have nine columns and the highest rank for each is 5, the highest possible score is $9 \times 5 = 45$. It is rare to have a 45, but in general, the higher your score, the more significant this activity is to you.

As you look over your totals, ask if there are some activities that have higher scores and that should have more of your time and attention. Are there other things that should have less? Talk about your conclusions with somebody who is spiritually mature and who knows you well.

8. You might want to repeat this whole process with additional questions. For example, you could have a column for the following:
   ‡ Does this activity help to advance my career?
   ‡ Does this strengthen my family?
   ‡ Does this activity make any potentially significant difference in the lives of others?

Ultimate questions. Regardless of all the above, there are several ultimate questions that must guide every activity in your life. You may think of others in addition to the following:

1. Do my activities build Christ's kingdom and honor him?
2. Are my activities motivated by the love of Christ?
3. Is each activity the best thing for me to do?
4. Do these activities make a difference?

Notes

CHAPTER 1: What Makes a Difference Maker?

[1]Details of the life of Susanna Wesley have been adapted from a book by Sandy Dengler, *Susanna Wesley: Servant of God*, (Chicago: Moody Press, 1987).

[2]This seems to be the opinion of Samuel G. Freedman in the book he wrote about Jessica Siegel and her high school: *Small Victories: The Real World of a Teacher, Her Students and Their High School* (New York: HarperCollins, 1990). The quotations in this section are taken from a review of Freedman's book: Chester E. Finn, Jr., "How a Good Teacher Burned Out," *Insight* 5, no. 25 (June 18, 1990): 62–63.

[3]Jesus' parable of the good Samaritan is recorded in Luke 10:25–37.

[4]In a letter to some of his supporters, evangelist Leighton Ford recently described a survey in which people ninety-five years or older were asked, "What would you change if you could live your life over?" The most common responses: They would reflect more, risk more, and *do more things that would outlive them*. Is this a way of saying they would try harder to be difference makers?

[5]Genesis 2:15; 1:28.

[6]Romans 5:8; 10:9; 1 John 1:8–9; John 10:10; 3:16; Matthew 28:18–20.

[7]Romans 12:4–8; 1 Corinthians 12; Ephesians 4:11–13.

[8]Ephesians 5:1.

[9]This is the view of Howard A. Snyder. His book *The Radical Wesley and Patterns for Church Renewal* (Grand Rapids: Zondervan, 1980) has supplied some of the material for this part of the book.

CHAPTER 2: What Are the Marks of a Difference Maker?

[1]Charles Garfield, *Peak Performers* (New York: William Morrow, 1986), 20. I mentioned peak performers in one of my earlier books but have raised it again because of its special relevance to difference making.

[2]The call of Moses is recorded in Exodus 3. Jonah's story is in the Old Testament book that bears his name. You can read about Gideon in Judges 6:33–7:25.

[3]2 Kings 5.

[4]1 Corinthians 1:1–3; 2:3–4.

[5]Acts 20:7–12.

⁶1 Corinthians 1:27–28.
⁷Genesis 50:20.
⁸Matthew 28:10–20.
⁹Isaiah 40:28–31.
¹⁰Proverbs 3:5–6; 16:9.
¹¹Luke 15:11–32.
¹²Luke 15:13, 30.

CHAPTER 3: What Hinders a Difference Maker?

¹Warren Bennis, *Why Leaders Can't Lead* (San Francisco: Jossey-Bass, 1989), 36.
²Adapted from a statement by Bill Hybels.
³2 Corinthians 8:17, 22; 9:2.
⁴Romans 12:11.
⁵Proverbs 19:2; Romans 10:2.
⁶Melvin Kinder, *Going Nowhere Fast: Step Off Life's Treadmills and Find Peace of Mind* (New York: Prentice-Hall, 1990).
⁷James 4:10. See also 1 Peter 5:5–6.
⁸Matthew 23:12.
⁹Warren Bennis, *On Becoming a Leader* (Reading, Mass.: Addison-Wesley, 1989), 5.
¹⁰Romans 12; 1 Corinthians 12; Ephesians 4.
¹¹Proverbs 11:14; 15:22; 20:18; 24:6.
¹²Philip B. Crosby, *Leading: The Art of Becoming an Executive* (New York: McGraw-Hill, 1990), 42.
¹³Deuteronomy 32:4; 2 Samuel 22:31; Psalm 18:30.
¹⁴Genesis 1:31.
¹⁵Proverbs 6:6–11; 12:24; 19:2; 28:20; 29:20.
¹⁶Colossians 3:23–24.
¹⁷1 Timothy 6:6–11.
¹⁸This quotation is from page 121 of the book we read in my class: Neil Postman, *Amusing Ourselves to Death: Public Discourse in the Age of Show Business* (New York: Penguin, 1985). For a disturbing report on the distortions of some television ministries, see *The Agony of Deceit: What Some TV Preachers Are Really Teaching*, ed. Michael Horton, (Chicago: Moody, 1990). See especially chapter 10, written by Quentin Schultze and titled "TV and Evangelism: Unequally Yoked?"
¹⁹Elton Trueblood, *While It Is Yet Day* (New York: Harper & Row, 1974).
²⁰Ezekiel 15; John 15:1–8.
²¹Bill Hybels, *Honest to God? Becoming an Authentic Christian* (Grand Rapids: Zondervan, 1990), 187.
²²Max DePree, *Leadership Is an Art* (New York: Doubleday, 1989), 99–100.

CHAPTER 4: Evaluate Your Thinking

[1]Richard Nixon, *In the Arena: A Memoir of Victory, Defeat and Renewal* (New York: Simon & Schuster, 1990), 230.

[2]Susan Champlin Taylor, "Everyday Heros: Meet Ten People Who Make a Difference Day In, Day Out," *Modern Maturity* 33, no. 3 (June–July 1990): 40–45.

[3]The quotations are taken from page 17 of Robert C. Girard's book *When the Vision Has Vanished: The Story of a Pastor and the Loss of a Church* (Grand Rapids: Zondervan, 1989).

[4]Girard, *When the Vision Has Vanished*, 45–46. This quotation is a good warning for successful churches and church leaders today.

[5]John 13:34–35; Galatians 5:22–23; Colossians 1:23; 2:6–7; Revelation 3:8.

[6]Colossians 2:6–7. See also James 4:10.

[7]Girard, *When the Vision Has Vanished*, 182.

[8]1 Corinthians 12:22; 2 Corinthians 12:7–10.

[9]Numbers 13:26–14:18.

[10]Isaiah 6:8.

[11]John 17:4.

[12]James 4:13–15.

[13]I am indebted to my friend Rowland Croucher in Australia for reminding me of these truths. See his *Still Waters, Deep Waters* (Sutherland, NSW, Australia: Albatross, 1987), 214.

[14]Matthew 20:26–27. The term servant-leadership probably was coined by Robert Greenleaf, an executive for AT&T. His book *Servant Leadership* was published in 1977 by Paulist Press.

[15]Matthew 23.

[16]Luke 10:37.

[17]Hebrews 6:10.

[18]Matthew 5:12; Hebrews 11:6.

[19]1 Corinthians 4:2.

[20]Matthew 22:37–39. See also Deuteronomy 10:12 and Micah 6:8.

[21]Mark 1:32–38.

[22]DePree, *Leadership Is an Art*, 73.

CHAPTER 5: Avoid Sinful Entanglements

[1]Psalms 6; 32:4; 38; 102:3–11.

[2]Psalm 143:8, 10.

[3]Erich Sauer, *In the Arena of Faith* (Grand Rapids: Eerdmans, 1955), 80.

[4]1 John 1:8–2:2; Matthew 18:21–22.

[5]Romans 3:23–24; 1 John 1:9; Galatians 5:22–23.

[6]See, for example, *Why Leaders Can't Lead* (San Francisco: Jossey-Bass, 1989); *On Becoming a Leader* (Reading, Mass.: Addison-Wesley,

1989); and the most popular, a book co-authored by Warren Bennis and Burt Nanus, *Leaders: The Strategies for Taking Charge* (New York: Harper & Row, 1985).

[7]This is the title of chapter 16 in *Why Leaders Can't Lead*. I have drawn from this book in writing some of the paragraphs that follow.

[8]Daniel 1:8; 6:10.

[9]Matthew 5:37; Ephesians 4:29; 5:10; James 1:22.

[10]Bennis, *Why Leaders Can't Lead*, 117. For a fuller treatment of integrity written from a Christian perspective, see Ted W. Engstrom with Robert C. Larson, *Integrity* (Dallas: Word, 1987).

[11]This is the observation of Lewis B. Smedes in *Caring and Commitment* (New York: Harper & Row, 1988). George Barna's research has led him to a similar conclusion. Currently "commitment is viewed negatively," he writes, "because it limits our ability to feel independent and free, to experience new things, to change our minds on the spur of the moment and to focus upon self-gratification rather than helping others. People willingly make commitments only when the expected outcome exceeds what they must sacrifice as a result of that commitment." This is from page 35 of Barna's book *The Frog in the Kettle: What Christians Need to Know About Life in the Year 2000* (Ventura, Calif.: Regal, 1990).

[12]Jerry Bridges makes an interesting observation on this tendency in *The Practice of Godliness* (Colorado Springs: NavPress, 1986), 93–94: "We evangelicals are not noted for our humility about our doctrines. . . . Whatever position we take in a specific area of theology, we tend to feel that our position is airtight, and that anyone holding a different view is altogether wrong. . . . Ironically, the more our views come from the teachings of someone else instead of from the Bible itself, the more rigidly we tend to hold to these views."

[13]Luke 18:14; James 4:10; 1 Peter 5:5–6.

[14]Isaiah 66:2.

[15]Acts 17.

[16]2 Timothy 4:13.

[17]Bennis and Namus, *Leaders*. Walter Anderson has written a delightful book about reading, *Read With Me: The Power of Reading and How It Transforms Lives* (Boston: Houghton-Mifflin, 1990).

CHAPTER 6: Pursue Clear Goals

[1]Hoshino Tomihiro, *Here So Close But I Didn't Know: An Autobiography of a Very Special Painter* (Tokyo: Kaisei-sha, 1988).

[2]Proverbs 16:9.

[3]This message, titled "Unleashing Our Potential," was presented at Willow Creek Community Church, South Barrington, Ill., July 1, 1990. I am grateful to Lee Strobel for permission to include the material that

follows, for his friendship, and for his personal encouragement to me as a writer.

[4]This is one message in the parable of the talents. See Matthew 25:23.

[5]The scores continued to be lopsided in subsequent games as the persistent Russians continued their tour.

[6]Malcolm Muggeridge, *Something Beautiful for God: Mother Teresa of Calcutta* (Garden City: Doubleday, 1971), 38.

[7]Hebrews 10:36; James 5:11; Revelation 2:2–3.

[8]Romans 5:3–5; James 1:3–4.

[9]This and the other quotations in this section are taken from Esther 4:14–16.

[10]Hebrews 1:2–3.

[11]Hebrews 4:13.

[12]Psalm 33:13–15; Matthew 6:28–33; 10:26, 33.

[13]Philippians 2:13.

CHAPTER 7: Focus Your Life on Christ

[1]Bridges, *The Practice of Godliness*, 43.

[2]John 17:3.

[3]Genesis 5:21–24; Hebrews 11:5.

[4]Jeremiah 9:23–24. Italics added.

[5]Some of what follows I have learned from the messages and books of Bill Hybels. See, for example, *Honest to God? Becoming an Authentic Christian* (Grand Rapids: Zondervan, 1990). For more difficult but very beneficial reading, see J. I. Packer's *Knowing God* (Downers Grove, Ill.: InterVarsity Press, 1973).

[6]Information about the Christian leaders' conferences is available by writing to Willow Creek Community Church, 67 East Algonquin Road, South Barrington, IL 60010.

[7]John 12:20–16:33.

[8]John 15:5, 8.

[9]Luke 6:46–47; John 13:34–35; 14:15.

CHAPTER 8: Expect Resistance

[1]I first read her story in "Minnie Pearl—A Gem of a Lady," *Arthritis Today* 4, no. 2 (March–April 1990). See also Sandra P. Aldrich, "More Than Giggles," *Christian Herald* 112, no. 1 (January/February 1990): 12–15.

[2]Hebrews 12:3, 7.

[3]Hebrews 12:4–11.

[4]The preceding paragraphs summarize Nehemiah 1–6.

[5]2 Thessalonians 2:1–2.

[6]Hebrews 10:32–39.

[7]This outline was suggested by *The Daily Walk* (December 16, 1989).

CHAPTER 9: Build Long-term Relationships

[1]Information on ServiceMaster is taken from the company's annual report and from a telephone conversation with Mr. Wessner.

[2]Hebrews 12:14–15. Throughout these chapters I refer to "the writer of Hebrews" because biblical scholars do not agree on the writer's identity. Most agree that it was not Paul. Barnabas and Apollos are often suggested as possible authors. Some have suggested that the writer was an unnamed woman.

[3]Jerry Bridges, *The Pursuit of Holiness* (Colorado Springs: NavPress, 1978), 15, 20.

[4]2 Timothy 2:21. See also Romans 6:19; 2 Corinthians 7:1; Ephesians 4:22–24; 1 Timothy 4:7; 1 Peter 1:15–16.

[5]1 Peter 1:15.

[6]Hebrews 12:14; 1 John 2:2–4.

[7]Gary R. Collins, *Christian Counseling: A Comprehensive Guide*, rev. ed. (Dallas: Word, 1988).

[8]Romans 12:18–20.

[9]See, for example, Hebrews 12:16; 13:4; 1 Corinthians 6:18; 2 Corinthians 12:21; Galatians 5:19; Ephesians 5:3; 1 Thessalonians 4:3.

[10]Galatians 5:22–26.

[11]Charles Colson, *Loving God* (Grand Rapids: Zondervan, 1983).

[12]W. Steven Brown, *Thirteen Errors Managers Make: And How You Can Avoid Them* (Old Tappan, N.J.: Revell, 1985).

[13]Genesis 25:29–34; Hebrews 12:16–17.

[14]Hebrews 12:16–17.

[15]The Gretzky Factor is mentioned on page 199 of a book by Warren Bennis, *On Becoming a Leader* (Reading, Mass.: Addison-Wesley, 1989). See also John Naisbitt and Patricia Aburdene, *Megatrends 2000: Ten New Directions for the 1990s* (New York: Morrow, 1990); Joe Cappo, *FutureScope: Success Strategies for the 1990s and Beyond* (Chicago: Longman Financial Services, 1990); and George Barna, *The Frog in the Kettle: What Christians Need to Know About Life in the Year 2000* (Ventura, Calif.: Regal, 1990).

[16]This was one finding in research by Denis E. Waitley and Robert B. Tucker. See their book *Winning the Innovation Game* (Old Tappan, N.J.: Revell, 1986).

[17]John 14:2–4; Acts 1:6–7, 11; Matthew 24:36.

CHAPTER 10: Look for Ways to Help Others

[1]Galatians 6:2.

[2]Hebrews 13:1, 3.

[3]Nouwen tells about this part of his spiritual journey in Henri J. M. Nouwen, *The Road to Daybreak: A Spiritual Journey* (New York: Doubleday, 1988).

[4]This is according to William Barclay, *The Letter to the Hebrews* (Edinburgh: The Saint Andrew Press, 1955), 218.

[5]Hebrews 12:18–29.

[6]Hebrews 13:2.

[7]Genesis 18 describes three angels who visited Abraham and Sarah; Genesis 19 mentions two angels who were entertained by Lot; and Judges 13 describes an angel who came in the form of a man to visit Manoah and his wife.

[8]Romans 12:13; 1 Timothy 3:2; 5:10; 1 Peter 4:9.

[9]1 Samuel 18:20–21; 19:11–17; 2 Samuel 6:16–23.

[10]Hebrews 13:4.

[11]Barclay, *The Letter to the Hebrews*, 221.

[12]Ventura, Calif.: Regal Books, 1978.

[13]Hybels, *Honest to God*, 80.

CHAPTER 11: Manage Your Resources

[1]1 Timothy 6:10; Matthew 6:24; Luke 6:24; Matthew 19:21–22.

[2]Philip Yancey, "Learning to Live With Money," *Christianity Today* 28, no. 18 (December 14, 1984): 30–42.

[3]Hebrews 13:5.

[4]Richard Foster, *Money, Sex and Power* (New York: Harper & Row, 1985), 5.

[5]Hebrews 13:5.

[6]Hebrews 13:5–6. See also Deuteronomy 31:6.

[7]Philippians 4:6–7; Hebrews 13:15–16.

[8]Mark 12:43–44; 2 Corinthians 8:12; 9:6–7.

[9]Foster, *Money, Sex and Power*, 76.

[10]The story of Mrs. Hill and her confrontation with Elizabeth was written by her husband. See Edward Victor Hill, "Unforgettable Jane Edna Hill," *Reader's Digest* (June 1990): 109–113.

CHAPTER 12: Select Good Mentors

[1]This quotation is from page 26 of Bob St. John's *The Landry Legend: Grace Under Pressure* (Dallas: Word, 1989). My description of Tom Landry Day, April 22, 1989, is adapted from this book.

[2]Hebrews 13:18.

[3]Hebrews 13:17.

[4]Ecclesiates 4:9–10.

[5]Ted Engstrom, *The Fine Art of Mentoring* (Brentwood, Tenn.: Wolgemuth & Hyatt, 1989), 34. For a brief but thoughtful discussion of

accountability see Jeff Jernigan, "I've Got You Under My Thumb . . . and Other Distorted Views of Accountability," *Discipleship Journal* 10, no. 6 (November/December, 1990): 10–14.

⁶For an excellent treatment of spiritual disciplines see Dallas Willard, *The Spirit of the Disciplines: Understanding How God Changes Lives* (New York: Harper & Row, 1988). The quotation is from Flora Wuellner and appears on page 22.

⁷Glandion Carney, *Heaven Within These Walls* (Ventura, Calif.: Regal, 1989), 169.

⁸I am grateful to my friend Devlin Donaldson of Compassion International for permission to use this story from his own golfing experience.

⁹Acts 2:42.

¹⁰2 Samuel 24.

¹¹Proverbs 11:14.

¹²Jim Spencer, "The Teacher Who Marches to an Up Beat," *Chicago Tribune* (May 29, 1986).

¹³Hebrews 13:9.

¹⁴2 Timothy 4:2–5.

¹⁵In a sad and sobering book that was mentioned in chapter 3, several astute writers have shown how some of the most prominent television preachers are guilty of teaching blatant heresy—and many do not even seem to realize what harm they are doing. See Horton, ed., *The Agony of Deceit*.

¹⁶Two recent, excellent books that are not dull are *Christians in the Crossfire: Guarding Your Mind Against Manipulation and Self-Deception* by Mark McMinn and James Foster (Newberg, Ore.: Barclay Press, 1990) and *Witch Hunt* by Bob and Gretchen Passantino (Nashville: Nelson, 1990).

¹⁷Matthew 7:15–23; Galatians 5:22–23.

¹⁸Passantino, *Witch Hunt*, 51.

CHAPTER 13: Commit Yourself to Prayer

¹Hebrews 13:18–19

²Donald G. Bloesch, *The Struggle of Prayer* (San Francisco: Harper & Row, 1980).

³This view is expressed in a very fine book on prayer by Bill Hybels, *Too Busy Not to Pray: Slowing Down to Be With God* (Downers Grove, Ill.: InterVarsity Press, 1988).

⁴I first encountered this idea in Lloyd John Ogilvie's book *Praying with Power* (Ventura, Calif.: Regal, 1983).

⁵Rowland Croucher, *Still Waters Deep Waters* (Claremont, Calif.: Albatross Books, 1987), 49, 147.

⁶1 Peter 3:18; Hebrews 9:26.

⁷Romans 12:1–2.
⁸Hebrews 13:15–16.

CHAPTER 14: Family Difference Makers

¹Mrs. Ponder received the Chicago Youth Center's second annual Adult Achievement Award on July 17, 1990. Her story was told in a newspaper article by Constanza Montaña, "Determined Mother of 8 Helps Her Kids Beat the Odds," *Chicago Tribune* (July 18, 1990).

²Some of this research is reported in an article by Carol Kleiman, "Personal Woes Top Drugs as Job Problem," *Chicago Tribune* (July 8, 1990).

³Genesis 12:4; Hebrews 11:8.
⁴Genesis 14.
⁵Genesis 16.
⁶Genesis 18:14; 22:14; Hebrews 11:13–19.
⁷Hebrews 13:5.
⁸Ephesians 5:33; 1 Peter 3:7; 1 Timothy 3:4; Ephesians 6:4; 1 Peter 2:17; 3:15.
⁹Matthew 7:3–5.
¹⁰Ephesians 4:15.
¹¹1 Peter 2:12, 15–16, 21, 23; 1 John 3:18.
¹²Engstrom, *The Fine Art of Mentoring*, 50.
¹³James 2:22–23.
¹⁴Matthew 20:20–27.
¹⁵Mark 10:45.
¹⁶1 Corinthians 12:7.
¹⁷James 4:10; 1 Peter 5:6.
¹⁸Titus 2:2–3.
¹⁹The topic of mentoring is discussed in more detail in chapters 12 and 15. For more information see Engstrom, *The Fine Art of Mentoring*.

CHAPTER 15: Community Difference Makers

¹Valerie Bell tells her own story in *Nobody's Children* (Dallas: Word, 1989).

²The story of Alberta is told on pages 191–192 of Gregg Albers' book *Counseling and AIDS* (Dallas: Word, 1990).

³1 Samuel 30.
⁴These questions are adapted from Hybels, *Honest to God?* 113, 139.

⁵The two Bennis "Laws of Academic Pseudodynamics" are in Bennis, *Why Leaders Can't Lead*, 15–16.
⁶Jeremiah 45:5.
⁷James 3:14–16.
⁸Galatians 5:20; Philippians 1:17; 2:3.

[9]Romans 15:20.

[10]1 Thessalonians 4:11.

[11]This is elaborated in more detail by Jerry Harvill, "Ambition: Vice or Virtue?" *Discipleship Journal* 10, no. 4 (July/August 1990): 12–14.

[12]2 Corinthians 5:9.

[13]Romans 12:2.

[14]Daniel J. Levinson, Charlotte N. Darrow, Edward B. Klein, Maria H. Levinson, and Braxton McKee, *The Seasons of a Man's Life* (New York: Alfred A. Knopf, 1978).

[15]Engstrom, *The Fine Art of Mentoring*, 4, 108.

[16]Engstrom, *The Fine Art of Mentoring*, 115.

[17]2 Corinthians 4:16–18.

[18]Acts 7:54–8:1.

[19]Philippians 3:17; 4:9.

[20]1 Corinthians 11:1. See also James 3:13 and 1 Peter 2:12.

[21]Douglas LaBier, *Modern Madness: The Emotional Fallout of Success* (Reading, Mass.: Addison-Wesley, 1986).

[22]The material for the preceding paragraphs is taken from an article by Billie Davis, "Don't Throw Bread From the Truck: and Other Lessons I've Learned About Helping People," *World Vision* 34, no. 4 (August–September 1990): 12–14.

[23]Thomas J. Peters and Robert H. Waterman, Jr., *In Search of Excellence: Lessons from America's Best-Run Companies* (New York: Harper & Row, 1982).

[24]Engstrom, *The Fine Art of Mentoring*, 116.

[25]Luke 14:28–29.

[26]Crosby, *Leading*, 8.

[27]Ecclesiastes 12:12.

[28]Joshua 1:1–9.

CHAPTER 16: Unusual Difference Makers

[1]Jeremiah 29:11.

[2]The book that includes Lloyd John Ogilvie's own account of his accident is *A Future and a Hope* (Dallas: Word, 1988).

[3]Judges 4–5.

[4]James 4:10; 1 Peter 5:5; Joshua 1:7–9; Matthew 20:26–28.

[5]From *The Reaper* (February 1962): 459. Quoted in J. Oswald Sanders, *Spiritual Leadership* (Bromley, Kent, England: Marshall Pickering, 1967), 21–22.

[6]One film series was made in conjunction with Dr. C. Everett Koop, who later became U.S. Surgeon General.

[7]George Barna, "How's Your Vision," *Discipleship Journal* 10, no. 4 (July/August 1990): 6–9.

[8]Bennis, *On Becoming a Leader*, 39, 6.

[9]Sanders, *Spiritual Leadership*, 48–51.

[10]Bennis, *On Becoming a Leader*, 83.

[11]It should be obvious that we are not using *visions* in the sense of apparitions, hallucinations, ghosts, night dreams, or supposed visits from angels or other supernatural beings from outer space.

[12]1 Corinthians 9:16–17; 2 Corinthians 5:14.

[13]Barna, "How's Your Vision?" 9.

[14]2 Timothy 3:12; 1 Peter 4:12–15.

[15]1 Samuel 16:7; 1 Corinthians 4:2, 5.

[16]Michael Korda, *Power! How to Get It, How to Use It* (New York: Random House, 1975).

[17]Alvin Toffler's thesis is advanced in his book *Powershift: Knowledge, Wealth, and Violence at the Edge of the 21st Century* (New York: Bantam, 1990).

[18]Foster, *Money, Sex and Power*, 176.

[19]Ephesians 6:12.

[20]I am grateful to Don Cousins of Willow Creek Community Church, South Barrington, Ill., for this timely insight and for his message "Standing Strong When Others Knock You Down," based on Daniel 6:1–10 and presented on July 26, 1990.

[21]The following paragraphs are adapted from Foster, *Money, Sex and Power*, 189–192.

[22]Colossians 2:15.

[23]1 John 4:4.

[24]Matthew 28:18.

[25]1 Peter 5:8.

[26]Luke 9:1–6.

[27]Galatians 5:22–24.

[28]2 Corinthians 12:9–10.

[29]The quotation that begins this paragraph and the story of the churches in Germany are from James R. Edwards, "The Fall and Rise of East Germany," *Christianity Today* 34, no. 7 (April 23, 1990): 16–18.

[30]1 Corinthians 1:26–30; 2:2–4.

[31]Daniel 1:3–4, 17, 20; 2:19–23, 27–28.

[32]Daniel 6:3–5.

[33]Daniel 6:10.

[34]2 Corinthians 3:6.

[35]Luke 1:6, 13–17, 26–39.

[36]Luke 1:38, 45.

[37]Robert Durback, ed., *Seeds of Hope: A Henri Nouwen Reader* (New York: Bantam, 1989), 105.

[38]Luke 1:38, 46–49.

CHAPTER 17: You Can Be a Difference Maker

[1] 1 Peter 1:24.

[2] James 4:17.

[3] Sanders, *Spiritual Leadership*, 50.

[4] John 21:17, 19.

[5] 2 Peter 3:18.

[6] These one sentence paragraphs are all taken from 1 Peter 1–2.

[7] A. W. Tozer. *The Pursuit of God.* (Camp Hill, PA: Christian Publications, 1982), 67. This book was originally published in 1969.

Index

277